Second Edition

World Link

Developing English Fluency

Susan Stempleski
Nancy Douglas
James R. Morgan

2

NATIONAL
GEOGRAPHIC
LEARNING

CENGAGE
Learning

Australia • Brazil • Japan • Korea • Mexico • Singapore • Spain • United Kingdom • United States

World Link 2: Developing English Fluency
Second Edition

Susan Stempleski, Nancy Douglas, and James R. Morgan

Publisher: Sherrise Roehr
Senior Development Editor: Jennifer Meldrum
Senior Development Editor: Katherine Carroll
Director of Global Marketing: Ian Martin
Senior Product Marketing Manager:
     Katie Kelley
Assistant Marketing Manager: Anders Bylund
Content Project Manager: John Sarantakis
Senior Print Buyer: Mary Beth Hennebury
Composition: Bill Smith Group
Cover/Text Design: Page2 LLC
Cover Image: iStockphoto

Library of Congress Control Number: 2009939402

Student Book ISBN-13: 978-1-4240-5502-9
Student Book ISBN-10: 1-4240-5502-4

Student Book + CD-ROM ISBN-13: 978-1-4240-6819-7
Student Book + CD-ROM ISBN-10: 1-4240-6819-3

National Geographic Learning
20 Channel Center Street
Boston, MA 02210
USA

Cengage Learning is a leading provider of customized learning solutions with office locations around the globe, including Singapore, the United Kingdom, Australia, Mexico, Brazil, and Japan.

Cengage Learning products are represented in Canada by Nelson Education, Ltd.

Visit National Geographic Learning at **ngl.cengage.com**

Visit our corporate website at **www.cengage.com**

Photo Credits: 2: center image copyright CURAphotography 2008/ Used under license from Shutterstock.com, top right bobbieo/iStockphoto.com, center right Photos.com , center left Creatas Images/Jupiterimages **3:** top left The Photo Works / Alamy, top left iofoto/istockphoto.com, top right Trista Weibell/iStockphoto.com, top right Oleg Prikhodko/iStockphoto.com **7:** center image copyright Adam Tinney 2009 / Used under license from Shutterstock.com, center left Laurence Gough/iStockphoto.com, center right Thinkstock/Jupiter Images **8:** top image copyright qingqing 2009/Used under license from Shutterstock.com, center pippa west/iStockphoto.com, bottom image copyright Felix Mizioznikov 2009 / Used under license from Shutterstock.com **9:** copyright 2005 PhotoDisc Inc., **10:** top right image copyright Francesco Ridolfi 2009 / Used under license from Shutterstock.com, center left Michael McDonnell/Hulton Archive/Getty Images, bottom left UPI Photo/Obama Press Office / Landov **12:** top left sébastien Baussais / Alamy, top center Kate Tero/danleap/iStockphoto.com, center right Niamh Baldock / Alamy, top right image copyright Faraways 2009/Used under license from Shutterstock.Com **13:** all images copyright 2005 PhotoDisc Inc. **14:** top right image copyright Gina Smith 2009 / Used under license from Shutterstock.com **17:** center right image copyright Tomo Jesenicnik 2009 / Used under license from Shutterstock.com **19:** Reuters/CORBIS **20:** top left image copyright Elena Elisseeva 2009 / Used under license from Shutterstock.com, top center Directphoto.org / Alamy, top right SGM/Stock Connection/Aurora Photos, bottom left Chang W. Lee /The New York Times **21:** Fausto Albuquerque / Alamy **22:** center right Courtesy of SWNS, bottom right Ever /iStockphoto.com **23:** © Iofoto | Dreamstime.com **24:** belknap/iStockphoto.com **27:** top left image copyright Yuri Arcurs 2009 / Used under license from Shutterstock.com, center right Todd Arena/iStockphoto.com, center left Larry Williams/Blend Images/Jupiter Images, top Joe Sohm/Visions of America LLC / Alamy **28:** Markus Divis/ Mac99/iStockphoto.com **29:** top right Jarno Gonzalez Zarraonandia/iStockphoto.com, bottom left image copyright Jarno Gonzalez Zarraonandia 2009 / Used under license from Shutterstock.com **30:** Jacom Stephens/iStockphoto.com **31:** center left AP Photo/Eric Gay, center JTB Photo/Japan Travel Bureau/PhotoLibrary, center right Ed Darack/Science Faction/Encyclopedia/Corbis **33:** top left image copyright Pamela Corey 2009/Used under license from Shutterstock.Com, top left image copyright Apollofoto/used under license from www.shutterstock.com, top right Ana Abejon/iStockphoto.com, top right image copyright Lev Olkha/used under license from www.shutterstock.com **34:** top left MR.SURAKIT HARNTONGKUL/iStockphoto.com, top Dale Berman/iStockphoto.com, top image copyright Denis Pepin 2009/Used under license from Shutterstock.Com, top right image copyright Josh Resnick 2009/Used under license from Shutterstock.com, center Andrzej Gibasiewicz/iStockphoto.com, center right Jonathan Larsen/iStockphoto.com, center right Jeremy Voisey/iStockphoto.com **37:** Gary Woodard | Dreamstime.com **38:** Jupiterimages/Pixland/Jupiter Images **41:** top left Maria Taglienti-Molinari/Hulton Archive/Getty Images, top right Pat Thielen / Alamy, center left Peter Beavis /Stone/Getty Images, center right image copyright AYAKOVLEVdotCOM 2009 / Used under license from Shutterstock.com, bottom left © Markfgd | Dreamstime.com, bottom right Scott Griessel/iStockphoto.com **42:** top left image copyright CREATISTA 2009 / Used under license from Shutterstock.com, top center Sorsillo | Dreamstime.com, top center Konstantyn| Dreamstime.com, top right image copyright andesign101 2009 / Used under license from Shutterstock.com **44:** image copyright Carlos E. Santa Maria 2009 / Used under license from Shutterstock.com **46:** top right Getty Images/Photos.com/Jupiterimages, center right Catherine Yeulet/iStockphoto.com **48:** top right SZE FEI WONG/iStockphoto.com, center right Ice | Dreamstime.com **49:** image copyright Monkey Business Images 2009 / Used under license from Shutterstock.com **51:** center left image copyright Rui Vale de Sousa 2009 / Used under license from Shutterstock.com, center © Aladin66 | Dreamstime.com, center right hfng/iStockphoto.com **53:** top right Digital Vision/Getty Images/RF, bottom right Alistair Laming / Alamy, **55:** Michael Klinec / Alamy **57:** Ben Blankenburg/iStockphoto.com **58:** © Tissiana | Dreamstime.com **59:** all images

Printed in the United States of America
6 7 16 15 14

Acknowledgments

Thank you to the educators who provided invaluable feedback throughout the development of the second edition of the *World Link* series: Rocio Abarca, Instituto Tecnológico de Costa Rica / FUNDATEC; Anthony Acevedo, ICPNA (Instituto Cultural Peruano Norteamericano); David Aduviri, CBA (Centro Boliviano Americano) - La Paz; Ramon Aguilar, Universidad Tecnológica de Hermosillo; Miguel Arrazola, CBA (Centro Boliviano Americano) - Santa Cruz; Cecilia Avila, Universidad de Xalapa; Isabel Baracat, CCI (Centro de Comunicação Inglesa); Andrea Brotto, CEICOM (Centro de Idiomas para Comunidades); George Bozanich, Soongsil University; Emma Campo, Universidad Central; Martha Carrasco, Universidad Autonoma de Sinaloa; Herbert Chavel, Korea Advanced Institute of Science and Technology; Denise de Bartolomeo, AMICANA (Asociación Mendocina de Intercambio Cultural Argentino Norteamericano); Rodrigo de Campos Rezende, SEVEN Idiomas; John Dennis, Hokuriku University; Kirvin Andrew Dyer, Yan Ping High School; Daniela Frillochi, ARICANA (Asociación Rosarina de Intercambio Cultural Argentino Norteamericano); Jose Gonzales, ICPNA (Instituto Cultural Peruano Norteamericano); Marina Gonzalez, Instituto Universitario de Lenguas Modernas; Robert Gordon, Korea Advanced Institute of Science and Technology; Gu Yingruo, Research Institute of Xiangzhou District, ZhuHai; Yo-Tien Ho, Takming University; Roxana Jimenez, Instituto Tecnológico de Costa Rica / FUNDATEC; Sirina Kainongsuang, Perfect Publishing Company Limited; Karen Ko, ChinYi University; Ching-Hua Lin, National Taiwan University of Science and Technology; Simon Liu, ChinYi University; Maria Helena Luna, Tronwell; Ady Marrero, Alianza Cultural Uruguay Estados Unidos; Nancy Mcaleer, ELC Universidad Interamericana de Panama; Michael McCallister, Feng Chia University Language Center; José Antonio Mendes Lopes, ICBEU (Instituto Cultural Brasil Estados Unidos); Leonardo Mercado, ICPNA (Instituto Cultural Peruano Norteamericano); Tania Molina, Instituto Tecnológico de Costa Rica / FUNDATEC; Iliana Mora, Instituto Tecnológico de Costa Rica / FUNDATEC; Fernando Morales, Universidad Tecnológica de Hermosillo; Vivian Morghen, ICANA (Instituto Cultural Argentino Norteamericano); Niu Yuchun, New Oriental School Beijing; Elizabeth Ortiz, COPEI (Copol English Institute); Virginia Ortiz, Universidad Autonoma de Tamaulipas; Peter Reilly, Universidad Bonaterra; Ren Huijun, New Oriental School Hangzhou; Andreina Romero, URBE (Universidad Rafael Belloso Chacín); Adelina Ruiz, Instituto Tecnologico de Estudios Superiores de Occidente; Eleonora Salas, IICANA (Instituto de Intercambio Cultural Argentino Norteamericano); Mary Sarawit, Naresuan University International College; Jenay Seymour, Hong-ik University; Huang Shuang, Shanghai International Studies University; Sávio Siqueira, ACBEU (Asociação Cultural Brasil Estados Unidos) / UFBA (Universidade Federal da Bahia); Beatriz Solina, ARICANA (Asociación Rosarina de Intercambio Cultural Argentino Norteamericano); Tran Nguyen Hoai Chi, Vietnam USA Society English Training Service Center; Maria Inés Valsecchi, Universidad Nacional de Río Cuarto; Patricia Veciño, ICANA (Instituto Cultural Argentino Norteamericano); Punchalee Wasanasomsithi, Chulalongkorn University; Tomoe Watanabe, Hiroshima City University; Tomohiro Yanagi, Chubu University; Jia Yuan, Global IELTS School.

Scope & Sequence

Unit/Lesson	Vocabulary Link	Listening	Language Link
Unit 1: All About Me			
Lesson A **The people in my life** p. 2 Lesson B **School days** p. 7	* **How do you know each other?** p. 2 *acquaintances, work together* * **I'm taking a class.** p. 7 *take a class, pass a test, get a good grade*	* **How do you know Michael?** p. 3 Make and check predictions Draw conclusions * **GBL Learning Center** p. 8 Listen for gist and details	* **The simple present vs. the present continuous** p. 5 * **Review of the simple past** p. 10
Unit 2: Let's Eat!			
Lesson A **Foods we like** p. 12 Lesson B **Eating well** p. 17	* **Street foods** p. 12 *fried, sweet, salty* * **What's their secret?** p. 17 *cut back, eat out, protect*	* **Foods of the southern United States** p. 13 Make and check predictions Listen for facts * **The Slow Food Movement** p. 18 Make and check predictions Infer information	* **The comparative form of adjectives** p. 15 * **The superlative form of adjectives** p. 20
Unit 3: Unsolved Mysteries			
Lesson A **What a coincidence!** p. 22 Lesson B **Mysteries of the world** p. 27	* **What are the chances?** p. 22 *luckily, unfortunately, take a chance* * **An unsolved mystery** p. 27 *mysterious, theory, prove*	* **Lucky you!** p. 23 Listen for gist Categorize information * **Full moon fever** p. 28 Use visuals to aid in listening Understand cause and effect	* **Stative verbs** p. 25 * **Modals of present possibility** p. 30
Review Units 1–3 p. 32			
Unit 4: Today's Trends			
Lesson A **Family trends** p. 36 Lesson B **Fashion trends** p. 41	* **Family trends** p. 36 *average, percent, twice as high* * **Fashion trends** p. 41 *conservative, sporty, casual*	* **Still at home** p. 37 Listen for main idea and details Determine a speaker's attitude * **You've got the look.** p. 42 Listen for gist and details Make and check predictions	* **Quantity expressions** p. 39 * **Giving advice with *could, should, ought to,* and *had better*** p. 44
Unit 5: Out and About			
Lesson A **Running errands** p. 46 Lesson B **This is my neighborhood.** p. 51	* **Handy Helpers** p. 46 *take a break, make an appointment, pick up/drop off* * **How's your commute?** p. 51 *running late, take a bus, stuck in traffic*	* **I'm calling because . . .** p. 47 Choose an appropriate response * **Commuters around the globe** p. 52 Listen for main idea and details Infer information	* **Polite requests with modal verbs and *mind*** p. 49 * **Intensifiers: *really, very, pretty*** p. 54
Unit 6: Student Life			
Lesson A **Starting out** p. 56 Lesson B **After graduation** p. 61	* **Applying to college** p. 56 *apply (to/for), competition, recommendation, get accepted* * **One of these days . . .** p. 61 *the day after tomorrow, in the near future*	* **Not your typical school** p. 57 Make and check predictions Draw conclusions * **Career Day** p. 62 Infer information Listen to sequence events	* **Plans and decisions with *be going to* and *will*** p. 59 * **Predictions with *be going to* and *will*** p. 64
Review Units 4–6 p. 66			

Pronunciation	Speaking & Speaking Strategy	Reading	Writing	Communication
Reduction of present continuous -ing ending p. 3	I'd like you to meet . . . p. 4 Introducing a person Responding to introductions	A book of memories p. 8 Skim for the main idea Summarize a text	The first day of class p. 11 Write about a time you attended a class for the first time	* Is it you? p. 6 Guessing classmates' identities based on their habits * Class awards p. 11 Selecting classmates to receive different awards
Sentence stress and rhythm p. 13	How about Thai food? p. 14 Making and responding to suggestions	The healthiest people in the world p. 18 Use the title and photo to make predictions Scan to find information and complete a chart	Restaurant review p. 21 Write a review of a restaurant you know	* Veronica's Restaurant p. 16 Creating a radio advertisement for an improved restaurant * Comparing foods p. 21 Creating a menu for a new restaurant
Past tense vowel shifts p. 23	I bet she's good at math. p. 24 Talking about possibility	Mysterious artwork p. 28 Use photos to make predictions Identify main ideas in paragraphs	A strange event p. 30 Write your own ending to a story	* Strange but true stories p. 26 Retelling a story and discussing possibilities * What's your theory? p. 31 Discussing theories of unsolved world mysteries
Unstressed of in rapid speech p. 37	I know what you're saying, but . . . p. 38 Disagreeing	Trendspotting p.42 Make predictions Understand text organization Draw conclusions	What's your advice? p. 45 Write a letter requesting advice	* What should they do? p. 40 Giving an opinion about what a person should do * Do you need a makeover? p. 45 Using a survey to determine your partner's trendiness
Reduced forms of could you and would you p. 47	I'd like to make an appointment. p. 48 Making appointments	Surprising neighborhoods p. 52 Use photos to make predictions Categorize information	Come to my neighborhood p. 54 Write about your neighborhood	* My benriya service p. 50 Creating an errand/chore service * Improving your community p. 55 Proposing a plan to make your community a better place
Reduced pronunciation of going to p. 57	Look on the bright side. p. 58 Offering another point of view	An opportunity of a lifetime p. 62 Make and check predictions Guess the meaning of words from context	My life now and in the future p. 65 Write predictions about your future	* Find someone who . . . p. 60 Talking to people about their plans for the future * Predicting the future p. 65 Using a profile to make predictions about someone's future

Scope & Sequence

Pronunciation	Speaking & Speaking Strategy	Reading	Writing	Communication
Reduced *want to* p. 71	**Do you want to go with me?** p. 72 Inviting someone to do something Accepting or refusing an invitation	**Get ready to get dirty** p. 76 Categorize information Guess the meaning of words from context	**In my country** p. 79 Write a description of a festival	* **Party planning** p. 74 Planning parties and deciding which one to attend * **An unusual holiday** p. 79 Inventing a new and unusual holiday
Was vs. *wasn't*; *were* vs. *weren't* p. 81	**So then what happened?** p. 82 Telling a story	**The Cinderella story** p. 86 Identify main ideas in paragraphs Scan for details	**A fairy-tale diary** p. 89 Tell a story from another person's point of view	* **Who's telling the truth?** p. 84 Listening to two stories and determining who is telling the truth * **Guess who I am** p. 89 Acting in English and seeing if others can guess who you are
Reduced *for* **in time expressions** p. 91	**Tell me a little about yourself.** p. 92 Interviewing for a job	**I love my job.** p. 96 Skim for the gist Summarize a text	**Writing about jobs** p. 98 Write about a job or a job interview	* **I really want this job!** p. 94 Role playing a real job interview * **Guess my job!** p. 99 Playing a guessing game to discover classmates' jobs
Repeating to clarify information p. 105	**May I speak to Lisa, please?** p. 106 Using the telephone	**Phone free in the car?** p. 110 Understand main ideas and supporting details Understand referents	**Opinions about cell phones** p. 112 Write your opinion about cell phones	* **Good news!** p. 108 Role playing a telephone call that brings good news * **How young is too young?** p. 113 Role playing a discussion about children and cell phones
Pronunciation of *s* **in** *used to* **and** *use / used* p. 115	**The fact is . . .** p. 116 Stating facts	**Rescue robots** p. 120 Understand a sequence of events Guess the meaning of words from context	**Comparing two products** p. 122 Write about two brands of the same item	* **Things have changed.** p. 118 Talking about how your life has changed in the last five years * **Design your own robot.** p. 123 Presenting your ideas for a new robot
Reduced *have to* **and** *has to* p. 125	**I can't remember where it is.** p. 126 Saying you've forgotten something	**Traveling alone** p. 130 Make predictions from titles and photos Find examples to support answers	**Travel experiences** p. 132 Write about a place you've visited	* **What should we take?** p. 128 Deciding what items to take on a camping trip * **Find someone who has . . .** p. 133 Surveying the class about their travel experiences

1 All About Me

Lesson A   The people in my life

1   Vocabulary Link   How do you know each other?

A   Mario is talking about four people in his life.
How does he know each person? Tell a partner.

> Cintra and I went out in the past, but she's not my girlfriend anymore. We're just friends now.

> I met Tomas and Silvia in college. We attended the same school. They both live in different cities now, but we're still close friends.

> Adrian and I work together. He's a nice guy, but to be honest, he's just an acquaintance. I don't know him very well.

Cintra

Adrian

Mario

Tomas

Silvia

B   In **A**, find a word or phrase in blue that has a similar meaning to each underlined word or phrase in the sentences in the chart. Write the word or phrase on the line. Compare your answers with a partner.

Words used to talk about ...		
friends	workmates	classmates
1. Cintra and I <u>dated</u> in the past. _went out_	5. We're <u>coworkers</u>. _Work together_	6. We <u>went to the same school</u>. _attended_
2. He's <u>someone I know, but not very well.</u> _acquaintance_		
3. We're <u>not dating</u> now. _just friends_		
4. We're still <u>good friends</u>. _close friends_		

C   Make a list of three people you know and then show your list to a partner. Tell your partner two facts about each person on your list.

> So, who is Yoon?

> He's a good friend. We went to high school together.

2 Listening How do you know Michael?

 A Look at the pictures below. How do you think the people in each picture know each other? Tell a partner.

 B Listen to the conversations and number the pictures in **A** in the order (1, 2, 3) you hear them. One picture is extra.

CD 1
Track 2

 C Look at your answers (1, 2, 3) in **B** and listen again. Which sentence is true about the people in each photo? Circle the correct answer.

CD 1
Track 2

1. a. They're dating.   b. They're acquaintances.   c. They're just friends.

2. a. They went to the same school.   b. They're just friends.   c. They're coworkers.

3. a. They're in the same class.   b. They're acquaintances.   c. They're close friends.

 D Look again at the pictures in **A**. Who are the people? How do they know each other? Tell a partner.

3 Pronunciation Reduction of present continuous -ing ending

  A Listen to the conversations. Notice how the underlined verbs are pronounced. Then practice with a partner.

CD 1
Track 3

1. **Clara:** Now I remember you. How are you <u>doing</u>?

   Rakesh: Fine. How about you?

2. **Lisa:** Hey, Josh. Are you busy?

   Josh: Yeah. I'm <u>writing</u> a paper for my English class.

   Lisa: OK. Talk to you later.

 B Practice reading the sentences below with a partner. Use the reduced pronunciation of -ing.

1. I'm trying to finish my homework.   3. She's working in her garden.

2. I'm fixing my car.   4. We're going to the movies.

 C Now listen and check your pronunciation.

CD 1
Track 4

UNIT 1 • All About Me   **3**

4 Speaking   I'd like you to meet . . .

CD 1
Track 5

A   Listen to the conversations. Who is meeting for the first time?

Conversation 1

Maria: Hi, Junko.

Junko: Hi, Maria. It's good to see you again! How are you?

Maria: Fine. How about you?

Junko: Pretty good.

Maria: Oh, and this is my friend Ricardo. We both go to City University.

Junko: Hey, Ricardo. Nice to meet you.

Ricardo: Yeah, you too.

Conversation 2

Mr. Otani: Morning, Miriam.

Miriam: Good morning, Mr. Otani. . . . Oh, Mr. Otani, I'd like you to meet Andres Garcia. He started working here yesterday. Andres, Mr. Otani is our V.P. of Sales.

Mr. Otani: Nice to meet you, Andres.

Andres: It's very nice to meet you, too, Mr. Otani.

ASK   ANSWER

What does Maria say to introduce Ricardo?
What does Miriam say to introduce Andres?

B   Practice both conversations with two partners.

5 Speaking Strategy

A   Work in groups of three: Student A, Student B, and Student C.

1. Student A: Choose a famous person to be. Write down your identity on a piece of paper and give it to Student B.

2. Student B: Read the identity of Student A. Then introduce Student A to Student C formally.

3. Change roles and follow steps 1 and 2 again.

Useful Expressions		
	Introducing a person to someone else	**Responding to introductions**
formal ↑	Mr. Otani, **I'd like to introduce you to** Andres.	It's (very) nice to meet you. (It's) nice / good to meet you, too.
	Mr. Otani, **I'd like you to meet** Andres.	
↓ informal	Junko, **this is** Ricardo. Junko, **meet** Ricardo. Junko, Ricardo.	Nice / Good to meet you. You, too.

B   Now introduce the "famous friends" you met in **A** to your other classmates. Use a formal or informal style.

Ana, I'd like you to meet _____.
(name)

It's nice to meet you, _____.
(name)

It's nice to meet you too, Ana.

6 Language Link   The simple present vs. the present continuous

A   Look at the pictures and read about Diane. Then use the words in the box to complete sentences 1, 2, and 3 below.

| fact   right now   routine   temporary |

Diane **works** in the sales department. She always **arrives** at work at 8:00 a.m.

Diane **is talking** on the telephone. She **is** also **typing** a report.

They need help in the finance department. Diane **is working** there this week only.

1. Sentence 1 states a general _____. Sentence 2 talks about a habit or _____. Use the simple present.

2. These events are happening _____. Use the present continuous.

3. This is a _____ situation. Use the present continuous.

B   Veronique Lesarg is a doctor. Use the simple present or present continuous to complete her profile.

My name (1) _____ (be) Veronique Lesarg. I (2) _____ (live) in Montreal. I (3) _____ (be) a pediatrician, a doctor for children. I usually (4) _____ (work) in a hospital, but these days, I (5) _____ (volunteer) for an organization called *Doctors Without Borders*. They (6) _____ (send) staff to other countries. This year, I (7) _____ (work) in Africa. At the moment, I (8) _____ (write) to you from a small village. There's no hospital here, so right now we (9) _____ (build) one.

> **Time expressions and the present continuous**
>
> Find and circle the three other time expressions used with the present continuous in the profile.

C   Complete these sentences to make questions in the simple present or the present continuous. Use the verbs in the box.

| do   eat   have   study   take   talk |

1. **A:** Why ___*are you studying*___ English ?
   B: I need it for my work.

2. **A:** _____ any other classes this term?
   B: Yes, I am—two business classes.

3. **A:** When _____ breakfast?
   B: About 7:00, usually.

4. **A:** How many brothers and sisters _____?
   B: Four brothers and one sister.

5. **A:** What _____ on the weekends?
   B: Play golf. And relax.

6. **A:** Who _____ to right now?
   B: Alex.

D   Now take turns asking and answering the questions in **C** with a partner.

7 Communication   Is it you?

A Take a sheet of paper and cut it into five strips.
On strips 1-3, write the following:

  1. a routine you never change

  2. an unusual habit

  3. a general fact about yourself

Continue your list.
On strips 4 and 5, write the following:

  4. an activity you are doing these days

  5. why you are studying English

1. I always get up at 5 a.m.

2. I sometimes eat peanut butter and tomato sandwiches.

3. I have a twin brother.

4. I'm learning to play the guitar.

5. I'm studying English because it's my major.

B Give your papers to the teacher. Your teacher
will mix up the papers and give you five new sentences.

 C Talk to your classmates.
Ask questions to find out who wrote each sentence.

 D Tell the class an interesting fact you learned about one of your classmates.

All About Me

1 Vocabulary Link   I'm taking a class.

A Read the statements and match each person with his or her picture below.
Then ask a partner: What is each person doing? Why?

1. "My parents think playing sports is important. So, after school, I have soccer practice every day. I also take tennis lessons for an hour on the weekend."

2. "I'm taking a class to prepare for the university entrance exam. The class meets for three hours a day. It's a lot of work, but I need help to pass the test."

3. "Two months ago, I was failing math—getting D's and F's. Now a tutor comes to my house and helps me with my homework, and I'm finally getting a good grade in the class!"

Erik

Marissa

John

B Complete the sentences with the correct form of the blue word(s) in **A**.

1. I can't go to the movies with you. I _____ baseball _____ this afternoon.

2. Tyler never studies, so now he is _____ a bad _____ in all his classes.

3. Maiko studied really hard and she _____ the test!

4. This term, I'm _____ two business classes at City University.

5. Our English class _____ on Tuesdays and Thursdays.

6. To _____ for tomorrow's class, please read pages 20 to 45.

7. My piano _____ is only for 30 minutes. After that, we can go to the store.

8. Liam _____ his biology class, so he has to retake it next term.

9. Nico is a _____ . He helps children with their homework.

ASK ANSWER

1. How are you doing in school? Do you get good grades?

2. Are you taking any special classes or lessons now (or did you in the past)? If yes, why? How often do (or did) the classes meet?

2 Listening   GBL Learning Center

A   Look at the places listed below. Why do people go to these places? What do they learn? Discuss your ideas with a partner.

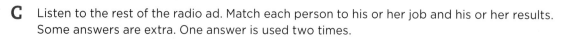

a language institute   a sports camp   a test preparation center

B   You are going to hear a radio ad. Listen. Which place in **A** is the ad talking about? What does the place help people do?

CD 1
Track 6

C   Listen to the rest of the radio ad. Match each person to his or her job and his or her results. Some answers are extra. One answer is used two times.

CD 1
Track 7

1.

2.

3.

a. doctor

b. engineer

c. soccer player

d. student

e. score went up 50 points

f. score went up 15 points

g. passed the first time

h. failed and then passed

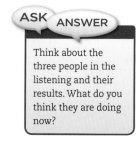
ASK ANSWER

Think about the three people in the listening and their results. What do you think they are doing now?

3 Reading   A book of memories

A   Skim the reading on page 9. Look quickly at the title, photo, and the first and last sentence in each paragraph. Then complete the sentence below.

A yearbook is _____ for a certain school year.

a. a list of the most popular students

b. a book used to prepare for exams

c. a collection of student photos and activities

d. a record of students' grades

B Read the article and check your answer in **A**.

Yearbooks in the United States

Most high schools in the United States publish a yearbook once a year, usually in the spring. It is a record of the school year—a "book of memories" for the students.

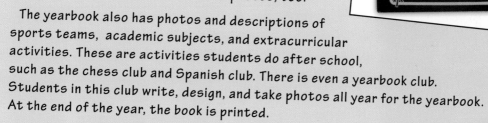

Inside a yearbook is each student's photo. The seniors are graduating soon, and their photos appear first. Next are the juniors. They are one year behind the seniors. Then come the sophomores, or second-year students. The last photos are the first-year students, the freshmen. The yearbook is not only about students. The teachers have photos, too.

The yearbook also has photos and descriptions of sports teams, academic subjects, and extracurricular activities. These are activities students do after school, such as the chess club and Spanish club. There is even a yearbook club. Students in this club write, design, and take photos all year for the yearbook. At the end of the year, the book is printed.

In the yearbook, some students receive special titles. The seniors vote and choose the "class clown" (a funny student), the "most likely to succeed" (a student who got the best grades), and the "best dressed" (a student with a good fashion sense). There are also other awards and categories.

Students usually sign each other's yearbooks. This is especially important for the seniors because they are graduating. Students write notes to each other, such as, "We had a lot of fun," or "I'll never forget you." They also write about all the fun and funny experiences they shared in school together.

C Complete the following summary using words from the article in **B**. Compare your answers with a partner.

A yearbook is a (1) _____ of the school year. You will find each student's (2) _____ in a yearbook. Photos of the (3) _____ come first. The yearbook features (4) _____ teams, academic subjects, and extracurricular activities. There are many clubs: the (5) _____ club makes the yearbook. Seniors vote and give some students (6) _____ such as "class clown." Students (7) _____ their classmates' yearbooks. The yearbook is truly a book of (8) _____ .

ASK **ANSWER**

Did/Does your high school have a yearbook? If yes, what is it like?
If no, would you like to have one? What would you put in your school yearbook?

4 Language Link   Review of the simple past

A Read about Diego's high school experiences. Underline the regular simple past verbs. Circle the irregular ones. Then tell a partner: what happened to Diego?

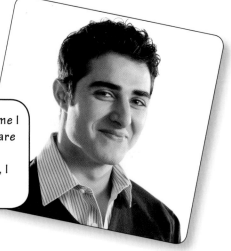

In high school, I <u>studied</u> a lot and (got) good grades. But the first time I took the university entrance exam, I failed. That was hard. To prepare for the next exam, I went to a test prep center. Two good things happened there: I met my girlfriend in the class. And the next time, I passed the entrance exam!

B Look at the high school photos of these two famous people. Complete each profile with the correct past tense verbs from the box. Then fill in their names.

act	become	die	go	take	write

Her mother (1) _____ when she was six years old. In high school, she (2) _____ drama and dance classes. She (3) _____ to New York in 1977, and later she (4) _____ a very famous singer. She also (5) _____ books for children and (6) _____ in movies.

Her name is (7) _____ Louise Ciccone.

be	divorce	enter	move	run	win

He (1) _____ born in Hawaii to an American mother and a Kenyan father. His parents (2) _____ and later he (3) _____ with his family to Indonesia and then again to the U.S. In 1988, he (4) _____ Harvard Law School and in 2008, he (5) _____ for President of the United States. He (6) _____ .

His name is (7) _____ _____ .

C Choose a person in **B** and write 3 or 4 questions about him or her. Then ask your partner the questions.

In high school, what classes did she take?

_____

_____

_____

_____

5 Writing   **The first day of class**

A   Think about your first day in English class. On a separate piece of paper, explain what happened on that day.

B   Exchange papers with a partner. Tell the class about your partner's memories.

I remember our first English class. I didn't know anyone. I sat next to Anika. She was really nice. When the class started, the teacher asked me a question but I got nervous and couldn't answer. Later, we played a game and I talked a lot.

6 Communication   **Class awards**

A   Work with a partner. Look at the awards below. Invent one more award for number 6.

1. Name: _____

2. Name: _____

3. Name: _____

4. Name: _____

5. Name: _____

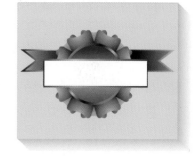

6. Name: _____

B   Who would be the best person in your class to receive each award in **A**? Write the names under the awards.

C   Tell the class your choices in **A**. Explain your reasons.

We chose Carlos as the "friendliest." On the first day of class, he said "hello" to everyone. He also helped . . .

 Check out the World Link video.

 Practice your English online at http://elt.heinle.com/worldlink

2 Let's Eat!

Lesson A   Foods we like

1   Vocabulary Link   Street foods

A   Read about these street foods. Which one(s) would you like to try? Why?

 -y = "full of something":
salty, spicy, oily, healthy,

_____ , _____

Street Foods
from around the World

Are you hungry and looking for a fast, inexpensive, and tasty snack? Here are three traditional street foods from around the world.

Paletas (Mexico)

What it is: A popsicle, usually made with juice or water and pieces of fresh fruit. Sometimes, red chili pepper is also added to a paleta. It's the perfect mix of sweet and spicy flavors!

Doner kebap (Turkey)

What it is: Pieces of juicy meat (usually lamb or chicken) served on a thin piece of bread with different sauces. It's delicious!

Maeng da (Thailand)

What it is: Water beetles (a kind of insect) are fried in oil and then salt is added. The result: a salty snack that tastes like potato chips!

Food • 27

B   Answer the questions below with a partner.

1. Read the note above. Then find two other adjectives in **A** that end in *-y*.

2. Choose four words from the note. Think of a matching food for each one.

C   What's your favorite street food? Tell your partner. Describe the food's taste.

> Near my house, you can buy churros on the street. They're fried pieces of dough with sugar added. They're sweet and delicious!

Describing how something tastes
This soup **is** tasty/delicious/terrible/sweet/salty/spicy.
This tea **tastes** good/delicious/terrible/sweet/salty/spicy.
This meat **tastes like** chicken.

2 Listening   Foods of the southern United States

A Look at the four photos below. What do you think each food tastes like? Tell your partner.

CD 1
Track 8

B Listen to Bill and Marta's conversation. Complete the information about the food.

(1) _____ chicken

grits

(2) _____ green tomatoes

(3) Mississippi _____ pie

Foods from the (4) _____ United States

CD 1
Track 9

C Listen to the rest of the conversation. Write the words used to describe the foods. Then circle the food Marta *didn't* like. Why didn't she like it?

1. The chicken was _____.

2. The grits tasted like oatmeal with a strong _____ flavor.

3. The tomatoes were _____, but they went _____ with the chicken and grits.

4. The dessert was a thick, _____ pie. It was too _____.

ASK ANSWER

Do these four foods sound good to you?
Why or why not?
Is your hometown (or region) famous for a special food? Describe it.

3 Pronunciation   Sentence stress and rhythm

CD 1
Track 10

A Listen and repeat the sentences. Note where the stress falls.

ORanges are SWEETer than GRAPEfruit.   PoTAto chips are SALtier than CRACKers.

CD 1
Track 11

B Circle the stressed syllables in these sentences. Then listen and check your answers. Practice saying the sentences with a partner.

1. Math is harder than English.

2. Apples are juicier than carrots.

3. The curry is spicier than the chili.

4. January is colder than February.

4 Speaking   **How about Thai food?**

CD 1
Track 12

A Listen to the conversation. Then answer the questions.

1. What are Jose and Jill going to eat for dinner?

2. How do Jose and Jill make suggestions? Underline the words.

Jose: So, Jill, where do you want to go to dinner tonight?

Jill: I don't know. Why don't we go to the pizza place on the corner?

Jose: Pizza again? I don't really feel like it.

Jill: OK, how about Thai food instead?

Jose: Fine with me. Where do you want to go?

Jill: Well, Thai House is near here. And there's another place — The Thai Cafe — but it's downtown.

Jose: Thai House is closer. Let's go there.

Jill: Sounds good!

B Practice the conversation with a partner.

5 Speaking Strategy

A Study the Useful Expressions. Then complete the dialogs below with a partner. Sometimes more than one answer is possible.

1. A: _____ stop at that cafe for coffee.
   B: Sounds _____!

2. A: What time do you want to meet in the morning?
   B: _____ meet at 7:00?
   A: That's a little early. _____ meeting at 8:00 instead?
   B: _____ with me. See you then.

3. A: What do you want to do today?
   B: _____ going to the beach?
   A: I don't _____ it. _____ see a movie instead.
   B: OK, _____ good.

Useful Expressions			
Making suggestions			**Responding to suggestions**
Statements			Great idea!
Let's	have	Thai food for dinner.	(That) sounds good (to me).
			Fine with me.
Questions			I don't really want to.
Why don't we	have	Thai food for dinner?	I don't really feel like it.
How / What about	having		

B Get into a group of three and do the following.

1. On your own: think of two restaurants that are good for a meal.

2. Suggest one of the restaurants to your partners. They can accept or refuse. If a person refuses, he or she should say why and suggest another restaurant.

3. Change roles and repeat steps 1 and 2.

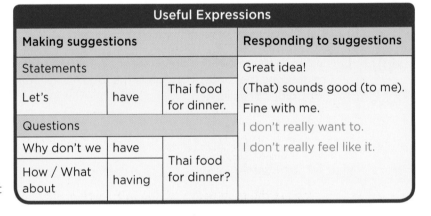

Why don't we go to Parr's Steakhouse for lunch?

That's a great idea!

I don't really feel like steak. How about having Indian food instead?

6 Language Link The comparative form of adjectives

A Read the advertisement. Underline all the adjectives. Then tell a partner: How are the underlined adjectives similar? How are they different?

ANNOUNCING . . .

GRAND REOPENING!!

JOE'S CHICKEN SHACK

Yes, we are open again! Come and see the improvements:
The portions were large . . .
but now they are **LARGER!**

Our spicy chicken is even **SPICIER!**
The seating area was spacious... but now it's **MORE SPACIOUS!**
Joe's Chicken Shack was good, but now it's **BETTER** than ever!

B Complete the chart with the missing words. Then check your answers with a partner.

The comparative form of adjectives					
One syllable		Two syllables		Three or more syllables	
_____	sweeter	simple	_____	_____	more refreshing
large	_____		spicier	delicious	_____
big	bigger	_____	more crowded	interesting	_____

 Notice! The comparative form of *good* is *better.*

C Complete the sentences with the comparative form of the adjective in parentheses.

1. The red curry is _____spicier_____ than the green curry. (spicy)

2. Cherry candy is _____ than real cherries. (sweet)

3. Wow! This apple pie is _____ than my Mom's! (delicious)

4. Our English teacher is _____ than our math teacher. (popular)

5. You're a _____ cook than I am. (good)

6. She is really embarrassed. Her face is _____ than an apple! (red)

i The comparative is often followed by *than* when comparing two things.

D Think of foods to compare using the adjectives in the box. Then say sentences comparing the foods with a partner.

> good   healthy   refreshing   salty   sweet

> Apples are healthier than potato chips.

 WORLD LINK

Hot bananas served with a spicy chocolate sauce is a popular dessert in...
a. Morocco
b. Guatemala
c. India

7 Communication   Veronica's Restaurant

A Look at the pictures of Veronica's Restaurant. Talk about the changes you see. Use the adjectives in the box to help you.

clean	new	happy
bright	big	cheerful
messy	old	dirty
good	bad	nice
beautiful		

The old Veronica's

> The old Veronica's was dirty.
> The new Veronica's is cleaner.

The new Veronica's

B With a partner, make a fifteen-second radio advertisement for the new Veronica's using your ideas from **A**. Write your ideas below. Then practice saying the announcement aloud.

_____

_____

_____

_____

C Present your radio advertisement to the class.
Whose was the best? Why?

> Come and see the new Veronica's!
> It's bigger and better than ever!

Let's Eat!

Lesson B Eating well

1 Vocabulary Link   What's their secret?

A Read the article below. Then answer the questions with a partner.

1. How are the five countries in the article similar?

2. Why are these people's traditional diets special?

Your Health

Mexico, Japan, Cameroon, Iceland, and Greece. What do these five countries have in common? In her book, *The Jungle Effect*, Dr. Daphne Miller says these places have some of the healthiest people in the world.

What's their secret? Dr. Miller says these people's traditional diets have important health benefits. The things they eat and drink increase their energy, help them think better, and protect against dangerous diseases like cancer.

Dr. Miller says a healthy diet and lifestyle are important. She says we should…

- eat more green vegetables, fish, yogurt, corn, beans, and spices.
- cut back on red meat and processed* foods.
- eat out in restaurants less.
- eliminate unhealthy habits, like smoking.
- get plenty of exercise.

*__processed__: instant (pre-made)

B Which statements would Dr. Miller agree with? Explain your answers to a partner.

1. People should eat more hamburgers.

2. Don't smoke.

3. Don't eat instant noodles too often.

4. Cook at home more.

5. Going to the gym once a month is enough.

6. Salmon, spinach, and black beans make up a healthy meal.

C Discuss the questions with a partner.

Do you have a healthy diet and lifestyle? Why or why not?

How often do you eat or drink the things listed in the article?

Word Partnership *diet*
balanced/healthy/unhealthy/
strict/traditional **diet**

2 Listening   The Slow Food Movement

A Discuss the questions with a partner.

1. We often hear about "fast food" and "instant food." What is it?

2. How often do you eat it?

CD 1
Track 13

B You are going to hear two people talking about the Slow Food Movement.

1. Which statements below do you think its members believe?

2. Listen and circle the correct answer(s).

 A **movement** is a group of people who have the same beliefs or ideas.

A **member** is a part of the group.

People should _____.

a. serve food slowly

b. eat no fast or instant foods

c. learn to prepare their own meals

d. grow food slowly and carefully

C Read the six statements below. Then listen again. For each sentence, choose *T* (true), *F* (false), or *NS* (not said). Explain your answer choices to a partner.

Mr. Moretti thinks . . .

CD 1
Track 13

	T	F	NS
1. most Slow Food members are Italian.	T	F	NS
2. eating a slow food diet is difficult for busy people.	T	F	NS
3. a slow food diet has many health benefits.	T	F	NS
4. a slow food diet is good for the environment.	T	F	NS
5. you should learn your grandparents' recipes.	T	F	NS
6. more stores are selling slow food items these days.	T	F	NS

ASK ANSWER

Would you join the Slow Food Movement? Why or why not?

3 Reading   The healthiest people in the world

A Look quickly at the title, picture, and reading on page 19. Then try to guess the answers to 1 and 2 below. Explain your ideas to a partner.

1. The reading is mainly about _____.

a. people from around the world

b. healthcare for older people

c. a group of people from Japan

d. older people in the United States

2. What is unusual about these people?

a. Most of them are women.

b. A large number live to age 100 or older.

c. They have the spiciest food in the world.

d. There are only 100 of them in the world.

B Now read the article and check your answers to 1 and 2 in **A**.

The Healthiest Lifestyle in the World?

In many countries around the world, people are living
5 longer than before. People have healthier lifestyles, and healthcare is
10 better, too.

Okinawa is an island off the coast of Japan. The people on Okinawa, the Okinawans, may have the longest lives and healthiest lifestyles in the world.

15 Researchers did a study. They started by looking at city and town birth records from 1879. They didn't expect to find many centenarians (hundred-year-olds) in the records, so they were very surprised to find so many old and healthy people living in 20 Okinawa. The United States, for example, has 10 centenarians per 100,000 people. In Okinawa there are 34 centenarians per 100,000 people!

What is the Okinawans' secret? 25 First, they eat a healthy diet that includes fresh fruits and vegetables. They also eat fish often and drink plenty of water and green tea. But researchers think that the Okinawans have other healthy habits as 30 well. They don't do hard exercise such as weight lifting or jogging. Instead, they prefer relaxing activities like gardening and walking. Researchers say that older Okinawans also have a good attitude[1] about 35 aging. They sit quietly and relax their minds with deep breathing exercises. They also enjoy massage.

■ ■ ■ ■ ■ ■ ■ ■ ■ ■ ■ ■

[1] **attitude:** the way you think or feel about something

C Scan the article and complete the chart below. You have two minutes.

Okinawan Centenarians

What they eat	What they drink
_____	_____
_____	_____
How they exercise	**How they relax**
_____	_____
_____	_____

ASK ANSWER

Why do Okinawans live so long?
Give some reasons.
Do people in your country have healthy lifestyles? Give examples.

4 Language Link The superlative form of adjectives

A Read the information about the restaurants. Then complete the sentences below with the correct form of each adjective.

A

opened: 1942
dinner menu: 40 euros

B

opened: 1925
dinner menu: 60 euros

C

opened: 1886
dinner menu: 80 euros

Restaurant A is _____old_____.

Restaurant B is _____than Restaurant A.

Restaurant C is **the oldest** restaurant.

Restaurant A is ___expensive___.

Restaurant B is _____than Restaurant A.

Restaurant C is _____most_____restaurant.

B Complete the chart with the missing words. Then check your answers with a partner.

The superlative form of adjectives		
One syllable	**Two syllables**	**Three or more syllables**
_____ the sweetest	simple _____	_____ the most expensive
large _____	_____ the spiciest	delicious _____
big the biggest	_____ the most crowded	interesting _____

> ⓘ **Notice!** The superlative form of *good* is *the best.*

C Complete the restaurant profile with the superlative form of the adjectives in parentheses. Then answer these questions:

1. Why is this restaurant unusual? Why do people like it?

2. Does it sound interesting to you? Why or why not?

Are you looking for an interesting place to have a meal? One of
(1) _____ (unusual) places in the world is Beijing's Dark Restaurant—
where you eat in a completely dark room! Dark Restaurant is one of
(2) _____ (trendy) spots* in China. For many, it is also
(3) _____ (popular) place to go on a first date. "It's
(4) _____ (good) way to get to know someone," says Zhi-ying
Chen, a visitor to the restaurant. "In the dark, you can relax and talk." Chen adds,
"I also had one of (5) _____ (delicious) meals of my life." His girlfriend agrees.
"It was (6) _____ (weird) but (7) _____ (interesting) eating
experience I ever had!"

spot = place

D Work with a partner. Use these adjectives to talk about restaurants you know.

noisy	trendy	cheap
boring	romantic	bad

> *Bob's Bistro is the noisiest restaurant I know.*

5 Writing   **Restaurant review**

A   You are a restaurant reviewer for a popular website. Choose a restaurant you know and make some notes. Then write a review.

Amazon Sun [★★★★★]

Amazon Sun is the best Brazilian restaurant in town. The food is delicious, the staff is friendly, and the prices are moderate. One of the tastiest dishes on the menu is the feijoada completa — a traditional dish of meat, beans, and Brazilian spices. It's excellent!

Amazon Sun is also one of the trendiest places to go these days, so be sure to make a reservation. Enjoy!

Restaurant: Amazon Sun

Food: Brazilian

Prices: Moderate

Location: Downtown

Service: Friendly

B   Read your partner's review. Do you want to try the restaurant? Why?

6 Communication   **Comparing foods**

A   Complete this chart with foods you know.

Spicy foods	Sweet foods	Expensive foods	Traditional foods

B   Compare your list with a partner's. Tell your partner which food you think is . . .

> I think tiramisu is the most delicious food on the list.

the most delicious   the most expensive   the hardest to prepare at home

the cheapest to buy   the healthiest   the worst for you

C   With your partner, create a menu for a new restaurant using many of the foods your group's members have written. Divide the menu into sections (appetizers, entrées, drinks, desserts). Include prices.

D   Post your menus for the class to see. Who has the best menu? Why?

Check out the World Link video.

Practice your English online at http://elt.heinle.com/worldlink

1   Vocabulary Link   **What are the chances?**

A   Look at the pictures and the title of the article below.
What do you think it's about? Tell your partner.

B   Now read the article. Then put the events of the story in order from 1–8.

____ Carmen read the letter.

____ The couple parted.

__1__ Carmen went to England.

____ Steve and Carmen got together again.

____ Carmen met Steve. They fell in love.

____ Years later, workmen found the letter.

____ Carmen's mother got the letter but then she lost it.

____ Steve wrote a letter to Carmen.

Letter reunites* lovers

In the mid 1990s, Carmen Ruiz Perez and Steve Smith met and fell in love. Carmen, from Spain, was studying in Steve's hometown of Devon, England. They dated for a year, but then Carmen got a job in Paris and the couple had to separate.

After Carmen left, Steve realized he still loved her. Did she love him? He took a chance and wrote a letter to Carmen's address in Paris. Unfortunately, she no longer lived there. Luckily, Steve had Carmen's home address in Spain. He sent a letter to her mother's house. Her mother got the letter, but it fell behind a piece of furniture in her house and was lost. Steve never heard from Carmen.

Several years later, workmen were fixing her mother's house and they found the letter by accident**. What good luck! Carmen read the note and contacted Steve. The couple met and soon married. Steve says he's lucky to have Carmen. "I missed my chance with her the first time. But in the end, everything worked out for the best."

By air mail
Par avion

* reunite: to bring two or more things together again

** by accident: by chance, without planning

C   Find a word or phrase in blue in the article that has the opposite meaning of each word or phrase in the chart. Compare answers with a partner.

word or phrase	opposite
reunite	
unfortunately	
on purpose	by accident
bad luck	
unlucky	
didn't try something difficult or risky	took a chance
ended badly	
had an opportunity to do something	missed a chance

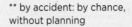

ASK **ANSWER**

Retell Steve and Carmen's story in your own words. Why was this couple lucky?

2 Listening   **Lucky you!**

A Discuss the questions with a partner.

1. Do you think you're a lucky person? Why or why not?

2. Do you ever do things for good luck? For example, do you wear a certain color or say special words?

CD 1
Track 14

B You are going to hear a man give a talk. Listen and choose the best title for it.

a. Good Things Happen . . . by Accident!

b. Why Are Some People Luckier Than Others?

c. Better Luck Next Time!

d. Beliefs About Luck Around the World

CD 1
Track 15

C Listen. Circle the correct answer.

1. Lucky / Unlucky people are very careful.

2. Lucky / Unlucky people take chances.

3. Lucky / Unlucky people listen to their feelings.

4. Lucky / Unlucky people focus on the facts.

5. Lucky / Unlucky people expect bad things to happen.

6. Lucky / Unlucky people expect good things to happen.

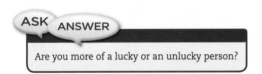

Are you more of a lucky or an unlucky person?

The Maneki Neko (or the "Lucky Cat") is often seen in homes, businesses, and restaurants around the world. It was first used in _____ .
a. China
b. India
c. Japan

3 Pronunciation   **Past tense vowel shifts**

A Complete the sentences below with the past tense form of each verb.

1. I _____ (hear) an interesting story on the radio last night.

2. Steve and Carmen _____ (meet) in England.

3. Later, she _____ (take) a job in Paris and they separated.

4. Steve _____ (know) he still loved Carmen so he _____ (write) a letter to her.

5. Carmen's mother _____ (get) the letter, but then she _____ (lose) it.

6. Later, workmen _____ (find) the letter and Carmen _____ (read) it. What luck!

7. I _____ (think) this was a good story.

B With a partner, say both the present and past tense of each verb in **A**.
What do you notice about the vowels in these verbs?

CD 1
Track 16

C Listen to the sentences in **A**. How was your pronunciation of the verbs?

D Practice saying the sentences with a partner.

4 Speaking I bet she's good at math.

CD 1
Track 17

A Nico and Sandra are talking about a news article. Listen and answer the questions.

1. What did a woman in New York City do?

2. How did she do it?

3. What is she going to do now?

Sandra: Anything interesting in today's news?

Nico: Yeah, I'm reading about a woman in New York City. She just won $25,000.

Sandra: That's a lot of money. Did she win the lottery?

Nico: No, she guessed the correct number of candies in a jar.

Sandra: Really? How many were there?

Nico: 7,954.

Sandra: Wow. That was a lucky guess!

Nico: Oh, I doubt she guessed. I bet she's good at math. The article says she won a similar contest in the past.

Sandra: So, what's she going to do with the money?

Nico: I don't know. She'll probably go on vacation or use it for school.

B Practice the conversation with a partner.

5 Speaking Strategy

A On the lines below, write two things about yourself that are true. Write one thing that is a lie.

_____

_____

_____

B Get into a group of 3-4 people and do the following:

1. One person tells the group his or her sentences.

2. The others . . .
   • ask the speaker questions to find out which sentence is a lie.
   • use the Useful Expressions to discuss their ideas.
   • guess which sentence is a lie. If you guess correctly, you get a point.

3. Change roles and repeat steps 1 and 2.

Useful Expressions: Talking about possibility	
Saying something is likely	
I bet (that)	Marco plays drums in a band.
Marco **probably**	plays drums in a band.
Maybe / Perhaps	Marco plays drums in a band.
To disagree that it is likely	
I doubt (that)	Marco plays drums in a band.

I bet Marco plays drums in a band. He owns a pair of drum sticks.

Well, maybe he plays drums, but not in a band.

Yeah, I doubt he plays drums in a band. I bet that's the lie.

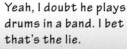

6 Language Link   Stative verbs

A Look at the chart of stative verbs below. Then add the verbs in the box to the chart.

> hate   hear   like   own   smell   understand

Stative Verbs				
Thinking verbs	Having verbs	Feeling verbs	Sensing verbs	Other verbs
believe	belong	appreciate	_____	seem
know	have	_____	see	look
think	_____	_____	_____	mean
_____		love	taste	cost
				need

B These sentences use stative verbs. The sentences in Column A are correct. The ones in Column B are incorrect. What can you say about stative verbs? Tell a partner.

Column A (correct)	Column B (incorrect)
I own more than 100 books.	~~I am owning more than 100 books.~~
We know many words in English.	~~We are knowing many words in English.~~
He seems like a nice person.	~~He is seeming like a nice person.~~

C Read the paragraphs below. If an <u>underlined verb</u> is used incorrectly, circle it and correct it. Then take turns reading the paragraphs aloud with a partner.

Winning the lottery—to most people, it <u>seems</u> like great luck. Unfortunately, for the winners, it's often the opposite. Ian Walters, for example, won a million pounds in a lottery in the UK five years ago. "When you <u>win</u> the lottery, suddenly you <u>are having</u> a lot of money," he explains. "You <u>are thinking</u> it will last forever, and you <u>spend</u> it quickly." And then one day, the money is gone. "Two years ago, I had a big house," Ian says. "These days, I'm <u>living</u> with my sister and I'm <u>working</u> in a small cafe. Luckily, I still <u>am owning</u> my car." So, what's Ian's advice? "In the past, I <u>believed</u> money could buy happiness," he says. "Now I <u>am knowing</u> this isn't true."

7 Communication **Strange but true stories**

A Work with a partner. Choose one story—Story A or Story B—below. Cover the other story up—do <u>not</u> read it. Read the story you chose. Think about answers to these questions as you read:

1. Who is the story about?

2. What happened?

Story A

David Brown and Michelle Kitson met in an unusual way. One night, David went out with his friends. The next morning, he woke up, thinking of a phone number. He didn't know whose it was, so he texted the person. "Did I meet you last night?" he asked in his message. In another town, Michelle got David's text. She didn't know him. She answered, "No. Who are you and where are you from?" David answered and the two continued texting. Finally, David took a chance and asked to meet Michelle. She agreed and now they are dating. David still can't believe his good luck. Why did he dream about Michelle's phone number? He still can't explain it.

Story B

On the morning of February 19, Corina Sanchez said goodbye to her husband and 17-year-old son and went to work. "It was a typical day," Corina remembers. "But then at lunchtime, I started to feel strange—really nervous—but I didn't know why. Two hours later, I got a phone call from my son—he was in a car accident!" Luckily, Corina's son wasn't hurt, but how did she know something was wrong? She still can't explain it.

B Work again with your partner and do the following:

Student A: In your own words, tell your story to your partner.
Student B: Listen to your partner's story. Take notes to answer the questions. Then switch roles.

1. Who is the story about? _____

2. What happened? _____

_____

C Can you explain what happened to David and Corina? Discuss your ideas with your partner. Then compare your ideas with another pair. Which explanation is the best?

> How did David know Michelle's phone number?

> Well, I bet he ...

Unsolved Mysteries

Lesson B   Mysteries of the world

"I first heard 'The Hum' in the 1970s. Only some people can hear it. There are lots of possible **explanations**: electrical wires, traffic noise, cell phone towers … I don't know what to think." —*Jaqui Moore, Australia*

1   Vocabulary Link   **An unsolved mystery**

A   Read the information below. What is "The Hum"? Who hears it? What causes it?

"I hear a low humming sound all the time. It sounds like a car engine. It's very **mysterious**. I hope someone **solves** this **mystery** soon because it's driving me crazy!" —*Alan Black, England*

"No one can **figure out** the source of the humming sound. We have a lot of **theories**, but no answers yet."—*Dr. Harini Gupta, scientist, India*

"We're **investigating** 'The Hum'. I can't even **prove** it exists because I can't hear a thing. But many people say that they hear it. It just doesn't **make sense**." —*Brian Lam, police officer, U.S.*

B   Match words 1–8 to their definitions (a–f). Some definitions match more than one word.

a. a guess or idea

b. to show that something is definitely true

c. to find an answer to a question or problem

d. to study something closely to find the truth

e. to be logical or understandable

f. strange or unusual

_____ 1. mysterious

_____ 2. figure out

_____ 3. make sense

_____ 4. explanation

_____ 5. investigate

_____ 6. theory

_____ 7. prove

_____ 8. solve

C   Write the noun or verb form of these words. Then compare your answers with your partner.

ASK   ANSWER

Look again at the theories in **A**. Can you think of other explanations for "The Hum"? In your opinion, which explanation makes the most sense?

Noun	Verb
_____	explain
investigation	_____
solution	_____
proof	_____

2 Listening — Full moon fever

A Look at the chart. What do you think it's showing us? Tell a partner.

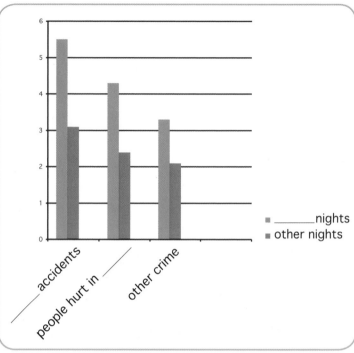

_____ nights
other nights

accidents
people hurt in _____
other crime

B You are going to hear a news report. Do the following:

1. Listen and complete the chart in **A**.

2. What are officials planning to do? Write your idea and then tell a partner.

_____

CD 1
Track 18

C Look at your answer to question 2 in **B**. Why are officials planning to do this? Listen to the rest of the report. Complete the sentences below.

1. The city needs more _____.

2. _____ nights are _____ than other nights.

3. More people _____.

CD 1
Track 19

> **ASK ANSWER**
>
> What are London officials planning to do? Why? Use your answers in **B** and **C** to explain.
>
> What are some beliefs about the moon in your country?

3 Reading — Mysterious artwork

A Look at the title and photos on page 29 and answer the questions below. Then read the interview once to check your answers.

1. What do you think the things in the photos are?

2. Who do you think made them?

B Read the passage again. Then write the questions below in the correct places in the interview. Two questions are extra.

- What was the purpose of the lines?
- How do the local people feel about the lines?
- What exactly are the Nazca Lines?
- Who created these unusual ground drawings?
- How did they do it—especially without modern technology?
- Can anyone visit the Nazca Lines?

MYSTERIOUS ARTWORK

Interviewer: The Nazca Desert in Peru is home to one of the most unusual sites in the world. In this issue, we talk with Dr. Gabriel Reyes about the Nazca Lines and why they are one of history's greatest mysteries.

So, Dr. Reyes, tell us: _____

Dr. Reyes: On the ground for almost 60 kilometers (37 miles) in the Peruvian desert are hundreds of line drawings of different animals, humans, insects, and other symbols. These drawings, known as the Nazca Lines, are very large. Some are over 200 meters (600 feet) long and can only be seen correctly from the sky.

Interviewer: _____

Dr. Reyes: For years, people had different theories. Some thought visitors from another planet drew them—maybe because the lines are best seen from a plane. Today, though, scientists believe the Nazca people created the images. They lived in the area from 200 B.C. to the 7th century A.D. and probably made the drawings over 1,500 years ago.

Interviewer: 1,500 years ago? _____

Dr. Reyes: Most likely they used simple tools. A team probably planned what they wanted a certain image to look like. Then they worked together and made the drawings in the desert ground. They didn't need planes or other modern equipment.

Interviewer: _____

Dr. Reyes: Good question. We still can't figure out why the Nazca people drew these large pictures on the ground – images you can really only see from the sky. Many scientists think the images might be religious symbols. Others believe the lines may be a large map; perhaps the Nazca people used the lines to find water in the desert. Still others think the lines were a special type of calendar. As I say, scientists are still investigating.

C The statements below are wrong. Change them so they are correct. Underline the sentence(s) in the interview that helped you make your changes.

1. North Americans probably created the lines in the year 1500 A. D.

2. The lines are small and must be looked at closely on the ground.

3. It was probably difficult for people to make the lines without modern tools.

4. Scientists now know what the Nazca Lines were used for—a calendar.

D Look back at the four questions in the interview. Take turns asking and answering these with a partner. When you answer a question, use your own words. Try not to look back at the reading.

4 Language Link   **Modals of present possibility**

A   Look at the picture and read the question and the answers in the chart. Then complete sentences 1 and 2 below with the correct modals.

1. Use _____ to say something is possible.
2. Use _____ to say something is not possible.

B   Read the note about short answers. Then complete the dialogs below. Practice them with a partner.

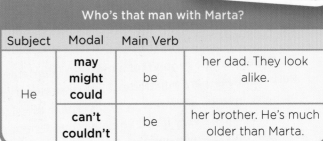

Who's that man with Marta?		
Subject	**Modal**	**Main Verb**
He	**may** **might** **could**	be	her dad. They look alike.
	can't **couldn't**	be	her brother. He's much older than Marta.

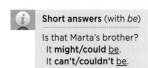

Short answers (with *be*)
Is that Marta's brother?
It **might/could** <u>be</u>.
It **can't/couldn't** <u>be</u>.

1. A: Is Luis from Brazil?
   B: He _____. He visits Sao Paulo all the time.

2. A: How old is Alice?
   B: I don't know. She _____ 30 or 35.
   C: She _____. She graduated from college in 1980.

3. A: Do you think "The Hum" is real?
   B: It _____. A lot of people hear it.

4. A: Where's Jane?
   B: I'm not sure. She _____ with Myra. They always hang out together.
   A: She _____. Myra is on vacation.

5. A: Are Yuko's parents in Japan now?
   B: They _____ there. I just saw them yesterday.

C   Read each situation. Think of two possible explanations for each one.

1. Your friend isn't answering her cell phone.
2. You received a mysterious package in the mail.
3. The teacher isn't here today.
4. A new student in our class is quiet.

5 Writing   **A strange event**

A   Read the paragraph on the right. Then write one or two more paragraphs to finish the story.

B   Exchange your story with a partner. As you read your partner's story, answer the questions. Then tell your partner your answers.

1. What was the sound Danny heard?
2. What is a good title for your partner's story?

> Danny woke up. "What was that noise?" he wondered. It was dark and Danny couldn't see. He turned on the light and looked at the clock. It was 2:00 a.m. Bang! There was the noise again. "What could it be?" Danny thought nervously. His parents weren't at home and his sister was at a friend's house. Danny opened his bedroom door and walked out to investigate. ...

6 Communication What's your theory?

A Look at the photos and read the notes about these unsolved mysteries. Then answer the question below about each.

The Chupacabra

The Yonaguni Monument

The Marfa Lights

What: It's a creature about 1.2 meters (4 feet) tall with red eyes and big teeth. It can jump high. It kills animals and drinks their blood. It's seen only at night.

Where: All over North and South America and parts of Russia

When: Was first seen in 1995

What: It's a large underwater rock formation—about 25 meters (82 feet) high. It looks like pyramids seen in Egypt and the Americas.

Where: In the Pacific Ocean, near Japan

When: Was discovered in 1986

What: They're lights that appear suddenly in the night sky. Often, there are two or three of them. They are about the size of a basketball. Sometimes they fly close to people's houses.

Where: In the desert near the town of Marfa, Texas (U.S.)

When: Were first seen in 1883

What do you think each thing is?

a. a large dog or other animal
b. a man in a costume
c. a terrible monster
d. your idea: _____

a. an underwater city
b. an old Japanese pyramid
c. nothing, just some rocks
d. your idea: _____

a. lights from a car or plane
b. some kind of strange weather
c. space aliens
d. your idea: _____

B Work in a group of 3 or 4 people. Discuss your answers to the question in **A**. Which is the most likely explanation?

> The Marfa Lights might be lights from a car or plane...

> No, they can't be because...

C Can you think of other unsolved mysteries like the ones in **A**? What do you think they are? Tell your group about them.

Check out the World Link video.

Practice your English online at http://elt.heinle.com/worldlink

Review: Units 1-3

1 Storyboard

A Susan, Maya, and Bruno work together. Look at the pictures and complete the conversations. For some blanks, more than one answer is possible.

B Practice the conversation with two people. Then change roles and practice again.

C Introduce a friend to another friend. Invite both friends out to dinner.

2 See It and Say It

A Below is a page from Anna Lopez's high school yearbook. She graduated in 1998. Read what her classmates wrote in her yearbook. How did Anna know each person? Discuss your ideas with a partner.

Sorry I didn't get to know you better, Anna. Good luck in college! Bobby

Hey, Anna! Best friends 4-ever! Rachel

Michael Evans   **Bobby Leong**   **Anna Lopez**   **Rachel Williams**

We're graduating, but you'll always be my girl, Anna. ~Michael

B Look at the people in **A** as they are today.

1. What are their relationships now?

2. Choose one of the pictures below. Make up a story about it. Answer these questions:
   • What happened to the people in your picture after high school?
   • How did they meet again?

3. Tell your partner the story of your picture.

Bobby and Anna

Rachel and Michael

3 Listening

 A Look at the photos below. What words would you use to describe these things? Tell your partner.

 B Four people are going to talk about their eating habits. Listen. Which food does each person like or eat a lot? Match a speaker (1, 2, 3, or 4) with the correct photo(s).

CD 1
Track 20

 C Read sentences 1–3 below. Then listen. Choose the correct answer for each sentence.

CD 1
Track 21

1. If you *get in shape*, you . . .

   a. gain weight.

   b. do things to be healthier.

   c. don't do much exercise.

2. If food tastes *bland*, it has . . .

   a. a strong taste.

   b. a lot of spices in it.

   c. no flavor.

3. If you *have a sweet tooth*, you . . .

   a. like sugary foods.

   b. can't eat sweets.

   c. are a good cook.

D Work with a partner and do the following:

1. Write three more food or drink items in the chart below.

food or drink item	Speaker 1	Speaker 2	Speaker 3	Speaker 4
1. pizza				
2. a glass of milk				
3. _____				
4. _____				
5. _____				

 2. Listen again. Which speaker (1, 2, 3, or 4) probably eats the items on your list often? Check (✔) the correct person.

CD 1
Track 20

3. Discuss your answers with a partner. Talk about the possibilities.

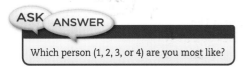
ASK ANSWER
Which person (1, 2, 3, or 4) are you most like?

I doubt that Speaker 1 eats pizza because...

4 Wonders of the World

Use the adjectives in the box to ask and answer questions about these monuments with a partner.

| beautiful | interesting | popular | strange |
| impressive | old | remote | tall |

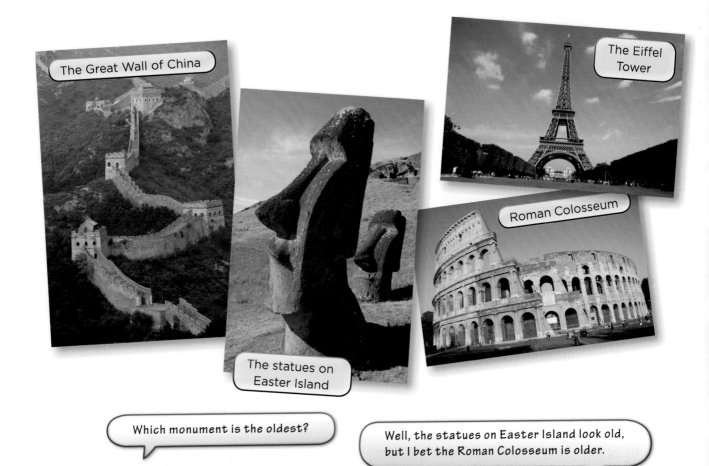

The Great Wall of China

The Eiffel Tower

Roman Colosseum

The statues on Easter Island

Which monument is the oldest?

Well, the statues on Easter Island look old, but I bet the Roman Colosseum is older.

5 I'm Reading an Interesting Book.

A Choose three words from the box. Write three sentences about yourself in your notebook. Use the simple present or the present continuous.

| eat | know | like | study |
| read | own | work | |

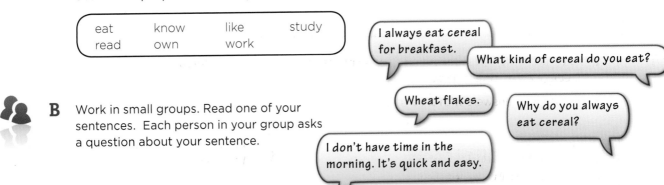

I always eat cereal for breakfast.

What kind of cereal do you eat?

B Work in small groups. Read one of your sentences. Each person in your group asks a question about your sentence.

Wheat flakes.

Why do you always eat cereal?

I don't have time in the morning. It's quick and easy.

1   Vocabulary Link   **Family trends**

A   Complete the sentences below with a word or phrase from the box. Compare your answers with a partner.

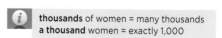

> **thousands** of women = many thousands
> **a thousand** women = exactly 1,000

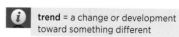

> **trend** = a change or development toward something different

*Trends
↓
Tendencias*

half	percent	thousands

American Family Trends

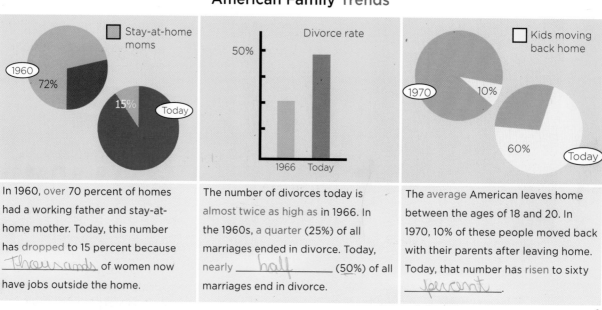

In 1960, over 70 percent of homes had a working father and stay-at-home mother. Today, this number has dropped to 15 percent because _Thousands_ of women now have jobs outside the home.

The number of divorces today is almost twice as high as in 1966. In the 1960s, a quarter (25%) of all marriages ended in divorce. Today, nearly ___half___ (50%) of all marriages end in divorce.

The average American leaves home between the ages of 18 and 20. In 1970, 10% of these people moved back with their parents after leaving home. Today, that number has risen to sixty ___percent___.

B   Find a blue word or phrase in **A** that has a similar meaning to each word or phrase below.

1. almost ___nearly___
2. more than ___over___
3. two times as high as ___twice as high as___
4. usual, typical ___average___

5. fifty percent ___half___
6. increased ___risen___
7. decreased ___dropped___
8. twenty-five percent, one-fourth ___a quarter___ 25%

C   Complete the sentences with a blue word in **A**. Which words are used to talk about an exact number or amount? Which talk about an approximate (not exact) amount?

1. Mary's birthday is next month. She's ___almost___ 12 years old. Aprox.
2. ___Half___ of 40 is 20.
3. There were ___thousands___ of people at the concert—maybe 20,000 or more.
4. Bob is ___over___ 30. Maybe he's 34 or 35.
5. Class A has 15 people and B has 30. Class B is ___twice___ as big as Class A.

> **ASK ANSWER**
>
> In your opinion, which trends in **A** are positive? Which are negative? Why?
>
> Are these trends similar or different in your country? Explain.

2 Listening · Still at home

A You will hear three people talking. Listen and answer the question.

What trend are the people talking about?

    a. people getting married later

    b. children living with their parents longer

    c. people having fewer children

B Look at your answer in **A** and read the questions below.
Then listen again and answer the questions.

1. In each place, what is causing this trend? Match the places with the reasons from the box.

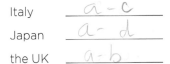

Italy	_a – c_
Japan	_a – d_
the UK	_a – b_

> a. Housing costs are high.   c. Getting a job is difficult.
> b. Education is expensive.   d. People are waiting to get married.

2. Which person does NOT think the trend is good?

    a. Alessandro   b. Aya   c. Evan

C Listen again and connect the information in the three columns.

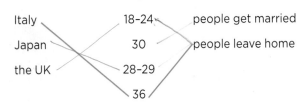

Italy   18–24   people get married
Japan   30   people leave home
the UK   28–29
         36

D Tell a partner about the trends in Italy, Japan, and the UK.
Use your answers in **B** and **C** to help you.

> In Italy, the average age that people leave home is 36. People wait to move out because …

3 Pronunciation · Unstressed *of* in rapid speech

A Listen. Notice the pronunciation of the word *of.*

1. Most of my friends still live with their parents.

2. A lot of people are getting married later.

3. Leaving your parents' house is part of becoming an adult.

> **Note:** In rapid speech, the final *f* sound in *of* is usually dropped before a consonant sound.

B Listen and complete the sentences. Then practice saying them aloud.

1. _____ the kids in my family still live at home.

2. _____ my friends are studying in New York City.

3. _____ people get divorced every year.

4. _____ them have children.

4 Speaking   **I know what you're saying, but . . .**

CD 1
Track 25

A Listen to the conversation. Then answer the questions with a partner.

1. Carla and her dad are fighting about something. What?

2. Who do you agree with—Carla or her dad?

Carla:	Dad, can I talk to you for a minute?
Dad:	Sure, what's up?
Carla:	Well, my friend Marta is going to see a concert tomorrow night and she invited me to go.
Dad:	Tomorrow night? But tomorrow's Tuesday. Sorry, Carla, but no.
Carla:	Dad! You *never* let me do anything.
Dad:	That's not true, Carla. You do lots of things. But the concert ends late and you have school on Wednesday.
Carla:	I know what you're saying, Dad, but it's just one night. And all of my friends are going.
Dad:	Sorry, Carla, but the answer is still "no."
Carla:	Oh, Dad, you're so unfair!

injusto

B Practice the conversation with a partner.

5 Speaking Strategy

Useful Expressions: Disagreeing	
Politely	**Strongly**
I know what you're saying, but . . .	That's not true.
Sorry, but I disagree. / I don't agree.	I totally / completely disagree.
I hear you, but . . . [very informal]	Oh, come on! / Are you serious? [very informal]

A Work with a partner. One person is the parent. The other person is the son or daughter.

1. Choose a situation from the box. Think of reasons for and against it.

2. Create a new conversation similar to the one above. In your dialog, use at least two Useful Expressions.

B Get together with another pair.

• **Pair 1:** Perform your dialog for another pair.

• **Pair 2:** Listen. Who do you agree with—the parent or child? Why?

C Switch roles and do **B** again.

> **Parents: Your son or daughter wants to . . .**
>
> • go on a date
>
> • visit another country by himself or herself
>
> • get a part-time job
>
> • your own idea: _____

6 Language Link   Quantity expressions

	all (of)
100%	all (of)
	most (of)
	a lot (of)
	some (of)
	a couple (of)
0%	none (of)

A   Read the information about six families from around the world.
Then write *all*, *most*, *a lot*, *some*, *a couple*, or *none* in the blanks below.

> ℹ️ a couple = two

	the SHAW family	the IKEDA family	the OLIVEIRA family	the CHOI family	the DEMIR family	the KUMAR family
hometown	Chicago	Tokyo	Sao Paulo	Seoul	Istanbul	New Delhi
language	English	Japanese	Portuguese	Korean	Turkish	English
housing	house	apartment	apartment	apartment	apartment	apartment
transportation	car	subway	bus	car	car	bus
wife works	restaurant	office	hotel	office	office	office
children	no	yes	yes	yes	yes	yes

1. _____ of the families live in big cities.
2. _____ of the families speak English.
3. _____ of them speak French.
4. _____ of the families live in apartments.
5. _____ of them own cars.
6. _____ of the families have a working wife.
7. _____ of the wives work in an office.
8. _____ of the families have children.

B   Complete the sentences below with the correct word(s).

> ℹ️ **Using of**
> (students everywhere) **Most students** work hard.
> (specific students) **Most of the students** in my class work hard.
> Not: ~~Most of students in my class work hard.~~

1. Most / Most of people want to be happy.

2. Most / Most of my friends speak English, but none / none of them speak it at home.

3. Some / Some of students live with their families because it's cheaper.

4. Most / Most of our neighbors have children; a couple / a couple of them have pets, too.

5. All / All of parents want their children to do well in school.

6. Some / Some of the teachers at my school are really strict.

C   Tell your partner about the families you know using *all (of)*, *most (of)*, *a lot (of)*, *some (of)*, *a couple (of)*, or *none (of)*. Use the list below.

have children   speak English

have a stay-at-home wife   own more than one car

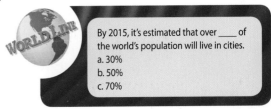

By 2015, it's estimated that over ____ of the world's population will live in cities.
a. 30%
b. 50%
c. 70%

7 Communication   What should they do?

A   Read each situation below. For each one, choose the answer you agree with or write your own idea.

> Luis has an older brother and sister. They both go to City University and Luis's father wants him to go there, too. Luis doesn't want to, but if he doesn't go to City, his father will not pay for his school. What should Luis do?

1. Go to City University like his father wants.
2. Start at City University and then later transfer (change) to another school. 3
3. Get a job, save his money, and pay for his own education. 1
4. Your idea: _Convince his father to go to another school._

> Yukiko's sixteen-year-old brother is hanging out with some bad people. He isn't going to class and he is fighting at school. Yukiko is worried about her brother. What should she do?

1. Wait a little longer. Maybe things will change.
2. Talk to her brother. Tell him her feelings. 3
3. Tell her parents about her brother.
4. Your idea: _Tell her another relative or friend._

> Josh is dating a girl named Holly. Josh loves Holly, but Josh's parents don't like her. This weekend is Josh's birthday. His parents are having a big party and they have invited all of his friends—except Holly. What should Josh do?

1. Talk to his parents and tell them to invite Holly.
2. Just bring Holly to the party. 2
3. Skip the party and spend the day with Holly.
4. Your idea: _Put her a wig and bring her to the party._

B   Get into a group of four or five people. Talk about your opinions in **A** with your group. Explain the reasons for your choice.

> I think Luis should go to City University.

> Yeah, I agree . . .

> Sorry, but I totally disagree with both of you. I think . . .

C   Look back at each situation in **A**. How many people in your group agreed with answers 1, 2, or 3? How many came up with their own answers? Compare your results with another group.

> Most of the people in our group think Luis should go to City University.

> Only one person in our group thinks Luis should go to City University. Most of us think . . .

A = 2 = 75%. 1 = 25%   B = 2 = 75%. 4 = 25%.   C = 2 = 50%. 4 = 50%.

Today's Trends

Lesson B Fashion trends

1 Vocabulary Link Fashion trends

A Read about some of these decades' popular fashions. Then, with a partner, use the words in blue to describe each photo on the time line.

 in = popular, fashionable
a look = a style

What was in?

The 80s

Conservative business suits with big shoulders for both men and women

Casual but sporty clothes known as the "preppy" look

Bright colors and big jewelry

Dramatic makeup and hairstyles and the color black—especially with punks and goths

The 90s

Grunge: a casual—almost sloppy—look of ripped jeans and old shirts

Hip-hop fashion: baseball caps, oversized shirts, and baggy pants

sloppy = mess

The 00s

skinny (fitted) jeans

Pointy shoes and boots for both men and women

Body piercings

Retro 80s fashion (dramatic hairstyles, bright colors)

B Discuss the questions with a partner.

1. What styles are "in" today? Describe each look.

2. Which words describe your look? What clothes do you usually wear?

> **Describing your look**
>
> casual / comfortable, colorful, conservative, dramatic, fun, retro, sloppy, sporty, stylish, unique

* Casual and comfortable, sporty

* Sporty clothes.   * Casual   * look very natural.

2 Listening　You've got the look.

A With a partner, describe the people's clothes in the photos below.

CD 1 Track 26

B Listen to a makeover TV show. Number the people (1, 2, or 3) that the speakers talk about. One picture is extra.

> If you **get a makeover**, you do things to make yourself more attractive.

CD 1 Track 27

C Look at your answers (1, 2, and 3) in **B**. Then do the following:

1. What style problem does each person have?
   Can you guess what the solutions are?

2. Listen to the rest of the show and complete the chart below.
   Use only one word per blank.

> **ASK ANSWER**
> Do you agree with the hosts' suggestions? Why or why not?

Style Problem	Style solution
Brad's look is too conservative / (sloppy.)	He could wear a ___nice___ new ___shirt___.
Tamara's clothes are too (baggy) / sporty.	She should wear something more ___fitted___, like a pair of ___skinny___ jeans and a fun ___top___.
Mimi's look is too casual / (mismatched.)	She should choose a single ___style___ and one or two ___colors___ that ___matched___.

3 Reading　Trendspotting

A Read the job advertisement. What do you think a *trendspotter* does? Who would hire a trendspotter?

> Are you between the ages of **15** and **22**? Do you like fashion and music? Do you know what's **hot**? You could be a **trendspotter!**
>
> - Try new products!
> - Participate in surveys!
> - Receive free samples!
>   Call now: 555-2200.

B Brooke is 18 years old. She works as a trendspotter. What does she do? Read her blog postings and check your answers in **A**.

Home   **About**   **Archives**   **Mail**   **RSS**

March 17

Part-time Job

💬 0 Comments | Posted by Brooke

Today I started my new part-time job as a trendspotter. I was nervous and didn't know what to expect. Well, guess what! It was a lot of fun! I'm telling all my friends, "You should think about becoming a trendspotter, too!"

This morning, we had to report to a recording studio by 10 a.m. The "Trends Coordinator," Mandy, explained the schedule. ~~then she gave us a tour of the studio~~ That was really cool!

Next we sat around a big table in a room. ~~there were about ten of us~~ Mandy gave each person three cards. One card said "Yes—All the way!" Another said, "It's OK." The third one said, "No way!" We listened to about 10 different songs. After each song, we had to hold up a card. They played some hip-hop, rock, heavy metal, and dance music. The heavy metal was "No way" for me!

March 24

Gifted

💬 0 Comments | Posted by Brooke

Do you know the rock group called "Gifted"? They're really popular right now. ~~Yesterday, they were here in the studio.~~ Too bad we missed them. Anyway, they have a new CD coming out on Jtunz soon. We saw six different CD covers. (I guess they are trying to choose one.) This time, we didn't have any cards. Instead, we just talked about the covers we liked. Mandy asked us questions: "Which ones do you like?" "Why do you like them?" "Would you buy a CD with this cover?"

We finished at 12:30. We meet again next week at a boutique downtown. We will look at some new fashions. Each week we go to a different location. Oh, and we also received a music gift card for our work. This "job" doesn't pay, but we get free stuff!

That's all for now!

C Check (✓) the sentence(s) Brooke would say about being a trendspotter. Compare your answers with a partner.

_____ It's kind of boring.

_____ You can make good money.

✓ You get free things.

_____ You work with famous people.

✓ People ask your opinion about lots of things.

✓ You work once a week at different places.

D Below are extra sentences from the reading.
Add each one to the correct place in the reading.
One sentence is extra.

Yesterday, they were here in the studio. ✓

I can't wait for our next meeting!

Then she gave us a tour of the studio. ✓

There were about ten of us. ✓

> **ASK / ANSWER**
>
> Why do you think companies use trendspotters?
> Do you think it's a good idea?
>
> Would you like to be a trendspotter? Why or why not?

4 Language Link Giving advice with *could, should, ought to,* and *had better*

A Read the question about cell phones and the three answers.
Then complete the sentences with the modal verbs in blue.

Q: I want to buy a new cell phone. What should I do?

A1: You **could** ask your friends or a salesperson for their suggestions.

A2: You **should** read *Consumer Advice* magazine. They rate the different phones.

A3: You**'d better** be careful. Some of the best cell phones are really expensive.

> *i* you'd better = you had better

In A1, _____Could_____ is used to make a suggestion (about two or more things).

In A2, _____should_____ is used to give advice. Ought to can also be used to give advice.

In A3, _had better_ is used to give stronger advice. It can sound like a warning.

B Complete the conversations with the expressions in the boxes.
Use each expression only once.

> *i* **Negative forms**
> You shouldn't wear a T-shirt to a job interview. It's too casual.
>
> We'd better not drive to the concert. It'll be hard to park.

> shouldn't   could   ought to

Betsy: I don't know what to wear to the party tonight.

Carla: You (1) _____Could_____ wear your new skinny jeans or black pants.

Betsy: It's a formal dress party.

Carla: Oh, then you (2) _____shouldn't_____ wear jeans. They're too casual.
You definitely (3) _____ought to_____ wear the black pants.

> had better   could   had better not

Fred: I still don't understand this grammar.

Doug: You (4) _____had better_____ get some help or you will fail the test. It's on Thursday.

Fred: Maybe I (5) _____could_____ take the test on Friday. That would give me extra time.

Doug: Well, you (6) _had better not_ delay. There's not much time!

C You are going to an informal party. Your partner is going to a formal party. Look at the list and give advice to each other.

> arrive a little late   wear casual clothes   bring a friend who wasn't invited
>
> bring food for the party   wear a suit or a nice dress   bring flowers or champagne to the host

> **You could wear a suit or nice dress.**

> **You shouldn't wear casual clothes.**

5 Writing — What's your advice?

A Read the post from Sad Sam in Seattle. What is his problem?

His appearance

B Now write a response to Sam. Give him some advice. Then share your writing with a partner.

*You could use different clothes
You should take of the cap and shave the beard*

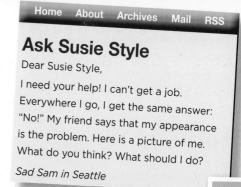

Ask Susie Style

Dear Susie Style,

I need your help! I can't get a job. Everywhere I go, I get the same answer: "No!" My friend says that my appearance is the problem. Here is a picture of me. What do you think? What should I do?

Sad Sam in Seattle

6 Communication — Do you need a makeover?

A Ask your partner the questions. Check (✓) your partner's answers.

How often do you . . .

	often	sometimes	never
1. wear "the same old thing"?		✓ 1	
2. buy something because it's cheap?			✓ 0
3. wear something comfortable but mismatched?		✓ 1	
4. wear something until it's completely worn out?		✓ 1	
5. leave the house without looking in the mirror?			✓ 0
6. read fashion magazines about new trends?		✓ 1	
7. change your hairstyle?			✓ 2
8. go to concerts and listen to new music?			✓ 2

⑧

B Calculate your partner's score. Use the table.

	for questions 1–5	**or questions 6–8**
often	score 2 points	score 0 points
sometimes	score 1 point	score 1 point
never	score 0 points	score 2 points

C Read the appropriate advice to your partner. What does your partner think of the advice?

0-3 points: You know what's "in" and have a great sense of style. Keep up the great work!	**4-7 points:** You have a good sense of style, but you could change a few things or just try to do something new every week.	**8-12 points:** Your look definitely needs an update. You could change something about your clothing or hairstyle. You should also try to go out more and see what's happening.	**13–16 points:** You scored a lot of points. You'd better think about getting a complete makeover!

Check out the World Link video.   Practice your English online at http://elt.heinle.com/worldlink

Do chores

1 Vocabulary Link **Handy Helpers**

A Read the ad below and answer the questions with a partner.

> **an errand:** a short trip you make to do or get something
>
> **a chore:** work you do regularly at home

1. What does Handy Helpers do?

2. Which items on the to-do list are errands?
   Which are chores? Write *E* for *errand* or *C* for *chore* next to each item.

Handy Helpers

Are you a busy person? Do you have too much to do—even on the weekends? Would you like more time to relax? If you answered "yes" to any of these questions, it's time to contact Handy Helpers!

We'll do your chores or run your errands so you can take a break. To learn more about us and the services we offer, call or e-mail us today!

Click here to **make a personal to-do list**

My to-do list
- ☐ take the dog for a walk
- ☐ go grocery shopping
- ☐ do the dishes
- ☐ sweep the floors and vacuum the rugs
- ☐ pick up the dry cleaning
- ☐ mail a package
- ☐ do the laundry
- ☐ take Marty to soccer practice
- ☐ make dinner

Other
- ☐ make an appointment to get a haircut
- ☐ make a dinner reservation at restaurant

B Complete the sentences below with the correct form of a word or phrase in blue from **A**.

1. All my clothes are dirty. I need to do the ___laundry___!

2. Kira's not home. She ___took___ her younger brothers ___to___ a movie.

3. My tooth hurts. I need to ___make an appointment___ to see the dentist.

4. The rug in the bedroom is dusty. Can you ___vacuum___ it?

5. Can you ___mail___ these letters at the post office?

6. I'd like to ___make a reservation___ for six people at 7:00 tonight. Is a table available?

7. Let's ___do___ the dinner dishes now.

8. Before you ___run___ any errands, you should ___make___ a list of the things you need to do.

9. Susan always ___pick up___ her children after they finish school.

10. I'm really tired. Let's ___take___ a ___break___. We can study again tomorrow.

C Which phrases in **A** use *do*, *make*, or *take*? Complete the chart below.
Can you think of other phrases that start with these words? Add them.

do	the chores, _____, _____
make	dinner, an appointment, _____
take	(the dog for) a walk, someone to a place, _____

ASK ANSWER

What chores or errands do you do?
When do you do them?

2 Listening — I'm calling because . . .

CD 1
Track 28

A You are going to hear four different phone calls. Read the sentences below. Then listen and circle the correct word(s) to complete each sentence.

 drop off: to bring and leave something somewhere; opposite = *pick up*

1. The woman is calling to make / change a reservation.

2. The man wants to know when he can drop off / pick up his dry cleaning.

3. The man is calling to make / change an appointment.

4. The girl wants her friend to take her to school / the doctor's office.

CD 1
Track 28

B Read the statements below. Then listen to each phone call again. What would the person in each conversation say next? Choose the best answer.

1. a. Yes, eight o'clock is fine. We'll see you then.

   b. No, sorry; but she'll call you back tonight.

   c. Sure. How's 7:30?

2. a. Great. I'll be in this afternoon.

   b. OK, thanks. I'll bring them in today.

   c. No, sorry. That doesn't work for me.

3. a. Yes, there are ten.

   b. Because I need to see the dentist.

   c. I'm sorry, but do you have something later?

4. a. OK, I'll see you at school later.

   b. Sure. I'll pick you up in ten minutes.

   c. Yes, it is.

ASK ANSWER

For what things do you usually make an appointment?

When you go to a restaurant, do you usually make a reservation?

3 Pronunciation — Reduced forms of *could you* and *would you*

CD 1
Track 29

A Listen to these sentences. Notice the reduced pronunciation of *could you* and *would you* in each sentence.

1. Could you open the window? It's hot in here.

2. Would you hold the door for me? Thanks.

3. Could you drop me off at school?

4. Would you help me lift this box?

CD 1
Track 30

B Listen to these sentences. Circle the words you hear.

1. That radio is really loud. Could you / Would you turn it down, please?

2. I think the computer is broken. Could you / Would you please look at it?

3. The phone's ringing. Could you / Would you answer it, please?

4. Let me see if he's in his office. Could you / Would you hold for a moment?

C With a partner, practice reading the sentences in **B**. Use reduced forms of *could you* and *would you.*

4 Speaking · I'd like to make an appointment.

CD 1
Track 31

A Listen to the conversation. Then answer the questions with a partner.

1. Why is Minh calling ISS Language Center?

2. When is he planning to go there?

Martina: Hello, ISS Language Center. This is Martina.

Minh: Yeah, hi. I'm in a TOEFL class that starts next week. I'd like to make an appointment to see the student counselor first.

Martina: Sure. I can help you with that. Let's see . . . can you come in tomorrow at 10:30?

Minh: No, that time isn't good for me. Do you have anything later in the day?

Martina: Let me check. . . . OK, how's 4:15?

Minh: That's perfect.

Martina: Great. Now, I just need to get your name.

Minh: It's Minh Nguyen.

Martina: Could you spell your last name for me, please?

Minh: Sure, it's N-G-U-Y-E-N.

B Practice the conversation with a partner.

5 Speaking Strategy

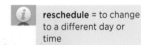

reschedule = to change to a different day or time

Useful Expressions: Making appointments		
Explaining why you're calling		
I'm calling to **I'd like to**	make an appointment to see a counselor.	
	make a dental / doctor's / hair appointment.	
	reschedule my appointment / our meeting.	
Scheduling the time		
Can you come in tomorrow **at** 2:00?	That's perfect. / That works great.	
Can you make it tomorrow **at** 2:00?	No, that day / time isn't good for me.	
How's / What about tomorrow **at** 4:00?		

A With a partner, read the situation below and create a new conversation similar to the one in Speaking. In your dialog, use at least two Useful Expressions.

Student A: You want to make an appointment to get a haircut on Thursday afternoon.

Student B: You're a hairstylist at a hair salon. The only appointment you have on Thursday is at 11:30 A.M. You have some afternoon appointments on the weekend.

B Switch roles. You and your classmate meet every Tuesday to practice English.

Student A: You need to reschedule your meeting for later in the week. Wednesday at 1:00 is best for you, but you can also meet on Friday.

Student B: You can only meet on Thursday or Friday after 1:00.

> Hi, Alex. What's up?

> I'm calling to . . .

6 Language Link   Polite requests with modal verbs and *mind*

A   Study the chart. Then read the short dialogs below and complete the sentences.

Making Requests		Responding to Requests
informal **Can / Will** you **Could / Would** you	help me, please?	OK. / Sure, no problem. / I'd be glad to. / Certainly. / Of course. Sorry, but . . .
formal **Would you mind**	helping me, please?	No, not at all. / No, I'd be glad to. Sorry, but . . .

1. **A:** Would you mind taking the dog for a walk?

   B: No, not at all.

   Speaker A's request is more formal in dialog 1 / 2.

   Speaker B says "No, I can't" to Speaker A in dialog 1 / 2.

2. **A:** Could you open the window?

   B: Sorry, but I think it's locked.

B   Find the error(s) in each dialog and correct them. Then practice the dialogs with a partner.

1. A: Can you spelling your last name for me, please?

   B: Of course. It's C-U-E-N-D-E.

2. A: The phone's ringing. Would you answer it, please?

   B: Yes, I would.

3. A: I can't go to class today. Could you take notes for me?

   B: No, I'd be glad to.

4. A: Would you mind to do the dishes tonight? I'm tired.

   B: No, not at all.

C   Write a request for each situation. Use the words in parentheses.

1. Your roommate is going grocery shopping. (pick up / some milk)

   _____

2. You didn't understand something your teacher said. (repeat / again)

   _____

3. You and your friend are leaving a party. Your friend drove, but you didn't. You're really tired. (drive / home)

   _____

D   With a partner, take turns making and responding to the requests in **C**. Refuse (say "no" to) one request and give a reason why.

> Can you pick up some milk, please?

> Sorry, but I'm not coming home first. I need to run errands. I'm afraid the milk will get warm.

7 Communication My *benriya* service

A Read the information below. Then tell a partner: What does a *benriya* do? Do you think it is a good service?

Need help or have a problem? Hire a *benriya*!

In Japan, a *benriya* is a person who fixes things, does household chores, and runs errands. *Benriyas* also do other annoying or difficult tasks for you. For example, they can . . .

- break up with your boyfriend or girlfriend
- talk to an angry friend, family member, or neighbor for you
- be your travel partner on a trip
- help you study
- listen to your problems and give you advice

B Work with a partner and create your own *benriya* service.

- What services do you offer (doing housework, running errands, fixing things, etc.)?
- How much do you charge for each service?
- What is your company's name and when do you work?

Company name: _hopful jobs_
Hours of operation: _9h — 5PM_

Service	Price
1. Take care of the kids	2$/h
2. Do braids	80 – 100$
3. cooking	30$/h
4. asistant	45$/h
5. sales perso/cashier	

C What things would you pay a *benriya* to do for you? List 2 or 3 ideas below.

D Get together with a new partner. Imagine you are calling his or her *benriya* service. Tell your partner what you need. Find out what he or she charges. Then switch roles.

A: Hello, Handy Helpers Service. How can I help you?

B: Yes, hello. I'm calling because I want to break up with my boyfriend. I need some help.

A: No problem! We can do that for you.

B: Great. Could you tell me how much you charge, please?

E Repeat **D** with three other partners. When you finish, ask your partners: Which *benriya* are you going to hire? Why?

Out and About

Lesson B This is my neighborhood.

1 Vocabulary Link How's your commute?

A Read the question and three responses. Then complete the chart below. Check answers with a partner.

The Question Lady wants to know ... How's your commute?

Tara

I often ride my bike to school. It takes about 25 minutes, but I like the exercise. If I'm running late, then I take the bus so I can get to class on time. By bus, it only takes about ten minutes.

Felipe

I live outside of Sao Paulo and I commute into the city every day by car. I'm often stuck in traffic for an hour or more, and that's no fun. For a short time, I took the subway to work, but that was worse. Sure, I could pass the time by sleeping or reading, but the crowded trains were terrible. Driving takes longer, but I prefer it.

Yoon

About a year ago, my company moved from Seoul to Pusan so now I've got a really long commute—about 227 km (142 miles). My wife and kids stay in Seoul, and every Monday morning I catch the bullet train to Pusan and spend the week there. On Friday nights, I go back to Seoul and spend time with my family on the weekend.

You can go or travel somewhere . . .	To go or travel somewhere, you can . . .
by bike, _____, _____, plane, subway, taxi, train. **on** foot. (= walking)	_____ your bike. **drive** your car. **catch** / _____ a bus, cab, plane, subway, train.

B Answer the questions with a partner.

1. How does each person in **A** commute (travel) to and from school or work?

2. Whose commute is the shortest? Whose is the longest?

3. Does it take Tara a long time to take the bus to school?

4. When Felipe took the train, how did he pass the time?

5. Does Yoon spend a lot of time with his family? Why or why not?

6. Your class starts at 10:00 and it's now 9:55. You're still at home. Are you running late or are you on time?

 It takes + time

It takes 30 minutes to bike to class.

It took 2 hours to do my homework.

It takes a long time to learn a language.

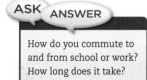

ASK ANSWER

How do you commute to and from school or work? How long does it take?

2 Listening   Commuters around the globe

A You are going to hear the first part of a news report. Read the questions below. Then listen and choose the best answer for each one.

1. The average person's commute is _____ one way.

   a. 40 minutes   b. one hour   c. nearly 2 hours

2. What question is this news show going to answer?

   a. Why are people's commutes getting longer?

   b. Who has the longest commute time in the world?

   c. How do people pass the time while commuting?

B You will hear four people giving an answer to question 2 in **A**. Read the statements below. Then listen and match a statement with a speaker. One statement is extra.

Speaker 1	3 I make plans for the day.
Speaker 2	4 I study or phone people.
Speaker 3	I read while I drive.
Speaker 4	2 I sleep or listen to music.
	1 I listen to stories.

C How does each person commute to work or school? Listen again and write the type(s) of transportation (bus, subway, bike, car, etc.) each person uses.

Speaker 1: by / on ___Car___

Speaker 2: by / on ___Subway___

Speaker 3: by / on ___Walk___

Speaker 4: by / on ___Subway/bus___

> ASK ANSWER
>
> How would you answer the question from the news report?
> Is your answer similar to any of the ones in **B**?

3 Reading   Surprising neighborhoods

A Look at the photos and the names of the cities and neighborhoods on page 53. Then read the statements below. Which neighborhood do you think each sentence describes? In some cases, both answers are possible.

1. To enter this neighborhood, you go through a gate.	Inwood	Fes-al-Bali
2. You can go to this neighborhood by subway.	Inwood	Fes-al-Bali
3. It has an old forest.	Inwood	Fes-al-Bali
4. You can see animals in this neighborhood.	Inwood	Fes-al-Bali
5. You can't drive cars here.	Inwood	Fes-al-Bali
6. It has a university.	Inwood	Fes-al-Bali
7. You can get lost here.	Inwood	Fes-al-Bali
8. Its streets are very narrow.	Inwood	Fes-al-Bali
9. Its streets are usually very crowded.	Inwood	Fes-al-Bali

B Kyle and Farid made web pages about their neighborhoods for a class project. Read about their neighborhoods. Were your answers in **A** correct? Make any necessary changes.

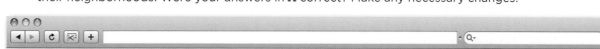

City: **New York City, USA** Neighborhood: **Inwood**

When you hear the word "Manhattan," what do you think of? Tall buildings, the Statue of Liberty, theaters, crowded streets? Well, all of those things are in Manhattan. My neighborhood—Inwood—is in Manhattan, too, but it's very different from the rest of the city. Why? Well, for one thing, there's a lot of greenery in this neighborhood. In fact, we have a forest in Inwood. Many of its trees are hundreds of years old and there are lots of small animals and wild birds. You can go hiking in some parts of it and get lost!

Many buildings in this neighborhood are old, too. For example, there's a farmhouse near my home. It's over 200 years old. Today it's a museum.

Inwood is an interesting neighborhood. It's a quiet place where you can hike in the parks. But then you can take a subway and, in 20 minutes, you can be in busy midtown Manhattan.

If you're ever in New York City, come and visit Inwood and see a part of Manhattan you didn't know existed. You'll be glad you did!

City: **Fes, Morocco** Neighborhood: **Fes-al-Bali**

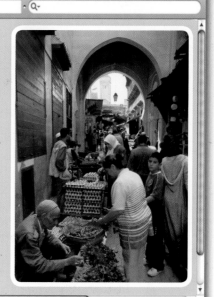

My name is Farid and I live in Fes-al-Bali—a neighborhood in Fes that's over 1,200 years old. You can find everything in my neighborhood—restaurants, shops, cafes, tearooms, and theaters. There are something like 10,000 businesses. We've also got one of the oldest universities in the world—the University of Al-Karaouine. It opened in the year 859.

The whole neighborhood of Fes-al-Bali is surrounded by a high wall with gates. You can drive inside the main gate, but once in, you can only travel through the streets on foot, by bicycle . . . or donkey! In fact, Fes-al-Bali is one of the largest car-free areas in the world. Still, the streets get pretty crowded—mostly because they're very narrow. Oh, and speaking of the streets, there are over 9,000 of them. It takes about 40 minutes to walk from one end of my neighborhood to the other, but be careful—the streets aren't straight. They're very long and winding and it's easy to get lost. Just last week I had to help some tourists from Australia.

If you're ever in Morocco, be sure to spend some time in Fes—and in my neighborhood, Fes-al-Bali. It's a place you'll never forget!

C Quickly scan the reading to find what each number describes. Write your answers. The first one is done as an example.

20: _the number of minutes it takes to go from Inwood to midtown Manhattan_

40: _____

200: _the age of_ _____

859: _____

1,200: _____

9,000: _the number of_ _____

10,000: _____

ASK ANSWER

How are these neighborhoods different from yours?

Which neighborhood would you like to visit? Why?

4 Language Link   Intensifiers: *really, very, pretty*

A Study the information in the chart. Then complete the sentences below with *really, very,* and/or *pretty*. Which sentences have more than one answer? Tell a partner.

	adverb	adverb	
I (don't) talk	really / very	loudly	in class.
I talk	pretty		

		adverb	adjective	noun
I (don't) have	a	really / very	long	commute.
I have		pretty		

	adverb	verb	
I (don't)	really	like	my new bike.

> *Really, very,* and *pretty* make adjectives and adverbs stronger.
>
> *Really* and *very* are stronger than *pretty.*
>
> *Really* can come before a verb. *Very* cannot.

1. I don't know Joan _____ well. Do you?

2. I usually take the subway to work. I don't _____ like to drive.

3. A: Who's that man over there?

   B: I'm _____ sure it's Leo, but I'm not certain.

4. That was a _____ good movie. I loved it.

> ⓘ You can use "at all" with negatives to mean "zero" or "never":
>
> I **didn't** like that movie **at all**.

B Unscramble the words and make sentences. Then tell a partner: Are the sentences true for you? If they aren't, change them so they are true.

1. busy / I / a / have / pretty / schedule   *I have a a busy pretty schedule*

2. live / I / noisy / really / in / neighborhood / a   *I live in a really noisy nei...*

3. don't / movies / really / scary / like / I   *I don't really like scary movie*

4. close / family / isn't / my / very   *My family isn't very close*

5. commute / it's / on / very / crowded / my   *My com...*

5 Writing   Come to my neighborhood

A Read the paragraphs on the right. Then tell a partner: Where does the writer live? What are the good things about his neighborhood? What are the bad things?

B Think about your neighborhood's good and bad points. Make a list of each. Then write two or three paragraphs about your neighborhood.

C Exchange your writing with a partner. Would you like to live in your partner's neighborhood? Why or why not?

> I live in a busy neighborhood in Seoul called Jamsil. There are good and bad things about living here.
>
> The best thing about my neighborhood is it's convenient. It's pretty easy for me to get to school by subway, bus, or cab. There are also a lot of stores and restaurants in my neighborhood, and there's a big park too. It's a great place to ride your bike or relax and it only takes five minutes to walk there from my house.
>
> The worst thing about my neighborhood is it's really noisy. There are a lot of big apartment buildings and I live on a pretty busy street. It's not the quietest neighborhood in Seoul, but I like living here!

6 Communication   Improving your community

A Cities around the world have different problems. Read about one city below. Then discuss the questions with a partner.

1. What is the city of Bogota doing? Why?

2. What do you think of the idea? Could it work in your city? Why or why not?

Problem: People in cities need open areas to exercise, but often there are too many cars and not enough parks.

One city's solution: Every Sunday from 7:00 A.M. to 2:00 P.M., Bogota, Colombia, closes its main city streets to cars and other motor vehicles. People can ride their bikes, walk, skate, play music, and spend time with friends and family on car-free city streets. The event helps people be healthier. Today, other cities around the world, including Melbourne, Australia and Quito, Ecuador, have similar events.

B With a partner, think of a problem in your city or neighborhood or choose one from the box below. Then think of at least one solution for the problem and explain why it's a good idea.

- Too many people commute to work or school every day by car.

- Children have no place to get exercise because there are no parks in my neighborhood.

- Your idea: _____

Problem: _____

Our solution: _____

_____

Why it's a good idea: _____

C Get together with another pair.

Pair A: Present your problem and explain your solution(s).

Pair B: Listen to Pair A's ideas. When they finish, answer the question below about their presentation. Explain your opinion to them.

What do you think of Pair A's idea?

- ☐ I really like the idea because . . .

- ☐ I kind of like the idea, but . . .

- ☐ Sorry, but I don't think the idea can work at all because . . .

D Switch roles and repeat **C**.

What is the most bike-friendly city in the world?
a. Amsterdam, Holland
b. Beijing, China
c. San Francisco, USA

Check out the World Link video.

Practice your English online at http://elt.heinle.com/worldlink

1 Vocabulary Link Applying to college

A Read the posting on the website. Then answer the questions with a partner.

1. What is Kento's problem?

2. Do you think Sergei's advice is good? Why or why not?

> ### Student Forums   Topic: Choosing a college
>
> I'm trying to choose a college. My family wants me to go to Tokyo University or Waseda University. They're two of the best colleges in Japan, but there's a lot of competition. Thousands of people apply to these schools every year, but they only admit a couple of hundred. It's a lot of work to get into these schools. And I'm not even sure I want to go to college right now! It's a really hard decision and I need some help!
>
> ~Kento (Tokyo, Japan)
>
> Hi, Kento: Some students get accepted to a school, but they're not really ready for university. Here's my recommendation: After graduation from high school, study abroad and improve your language skills, or apply for an internship* for a year. Later, when you're ready for college, you can show how your "year off" prepared you for university. Good luck!
>
> ~Sergei (Moscow, Russia)
>
> *internship: a job, usually done for a short time, in which you learn about a certain type of work

B Complete the chart with a word in blue from **A**. Then use the correct form of a word in the chart to complete the sentences below.

Verb	Noun
_____	admission
_____ (to/for)	application
compete	_____
decide	_____
graduate	_____
recommend	_____

> The suffixes **-ion, -ation, -ition**, and **-sion** change verbs into nouns.
>
> graduate + ion = graduat*ion*
>
> recommend + ation = recommend*ation*
>
> compete + ition = compet*ition*
>
> decide + sion = deci*sion*

1. My brother _____ from Oxford University last year.

2. If you want to go to IES Language School, you can _____ online, or they will mail a(n) _____ to you.

3. These days, there's a lot of _____ for jobs. For one job, we interviewed over 100 people!

4. Leo got into Harvard and Yale, but he can't _____ which university is better.

5. Wesley College _____ students twice a year—you can enter in August or January.

6. I'm new to this neighborhood. Can you _____ a good place to eat?

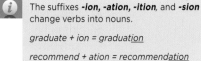

ASK ANSWER

How many universities are you going to (or did you) apply to? Did you get into them?

Can you recommend a good place to study English?

2 Listening   **Not your typical school**

A You're going to hear an interview about a special school. Look at the profile below. Why do you think Stratton Mountain School is special? Tell a partner.

CD 1
Track 34

B A student is going to talk about the school below. Listen and complete the profile.
Use only one word per blank.

> **School Profile**
>
> **Name:** Stratton Mountain School (for students ages _____ to _____)
>
> **Where:** Vermont, USA
>
> **Students:** Most are _____ and snowboarders.
>
> After graduation, many compete in the Winter _____
>
> **A typical day at Stratton:**
>
> 7:00 A.M.: _____
>
> 8:00 A.M. to _____: Students are in _____.
>
> 12:30 to 5:00 P.M.: Students have _____.

C Review your notes in **B**. Then tell a partner: Why is Stratton an unusual high school?

CD 1
Track 35

D Read sentences 1–3 below. Then listen again. Choose the correct answer for each one.

1. A *coed* school admits . . .
   A: boys only.
   B: girls only.
   C: both boys and girls.

2. A *dorm* is a type of student . . .
   A: activity.
   B: housing.
   C: training.

3. A school's *alumni* are . . .
   A: graduates from the school.
   B: students now at the school.
   C: teachers at the school.

ASK ANSWER

Do you think Stratton is an interesting school? Why or why not?

3 Pronunciation   **Reduced pronunciation of *going to***

CD 1
Track 36

A Listen to the sentences. Notice the reduced pronunciation of *going to* in each sentence.

1. I'm going to apply to three colleges.
2. He's going to clean the house next week.
3. We're going to study together for the big exam.
4. They're not going to finish in time.

CD 1
Track 37

B Listen to the sentences and write the missing words you hear.

1. _____ meet them before 3:00.
2. _____ take a vacation this summer.
3. _____ call us tomorrow.
4. _____ attend Harvard University.

C Take turns saying the sentences in **A** and **B** with a partner.

4 Speaking   **Look on the bright side.**

CD 1
Track 38

A Listen to the conversation. Then answer the questions with a partner.

1. Tom is unhappy about something. What?

2. How does Hans make Tom feel better? Underline Hans's advice.

3. What do you think "look on the bright side" means?

Hans: Hey, Tom. How's it going with the college applications?

Tom: So-so. I didn't get into McGill University.

Hans: Really? Sorry to hear that. Did you apply to any other schools?

Tom: Yeah, three others.

Hans: And?

Tom: I got into all of them.

Hans: Well, that's great!

Tom: Yeah, but I really wanted to go to McGill.

Hans: Well, look on the bright side—three other schools accepted you.

Tom: Yeah, I guess you're right.

Hans: So, which school are you going to attend?

Tom: I'm not sure. Maybe I'll go to Queen's University.

B Practice the conversation with a partner.

5 Speaking Strategy

Useful Expressions: Offering another point of view	
I didn't get accepted to McGill University.	
Look on the bright side . . . Well, the good news is . . . Look at it this way . . . Yes, but on the other hand . . . (Yes, but) then again . . .	three other schools accepted you.

A Read the problems. For each, add one more "positive" point of view to the chart.

The problem	A positive point of view
You applied to two English schools: one in the UK and one in Australia. You really wanted to study in the UK, but only the school in Australia accepted you.	1. You got accepted to a good school. 2. _____
You're invited to a party at the beach. You're not sure if you want to go. You're worried you won't know many people.	1. You can meet new people. 2. _____

B Choose one situation from **A**. With a partner, create a short conversation like the one in Speaking. Use the Useful Expressions in your dialog.

C Change roles. Use the other situation and repeat **B**.

6 Language Link   Plans and decisions with *be going to* and *will*

A   Read these conversations. Then complete sentences 1 and 2 below.

Ana: I got accepted to college.

Pablo: Congratulations!

Ana: Thanks. I'm going to attend McGill University in the fall.

Yuri: I want to register for the grammar class.

Advisor: I'm sorry. That class is full.

Yuri: OK. I'll register for the writing class, then.

1. Ana uses *be going to* to talk about . . .

☐ a. a sudden decision.

☐ b. a plan she already made.

2. Yuri uses *will* ('ll) to talk about . . .

☐ a. a sudden decision.

☐ b. a plan he already made.

B   Complete the sentences with *be going to* or *will*. Then check your answers with a partner.

1. I graduate from high school in June. Then I _____ attend college in the fall.

2. I'm bored and don't know what to do. Wait, I know . . . I _____ read and watch TV.

3. Waiter: What would you like today?
   Customer: Let's see . . . I _____ have the chicken and rice, please.

4. I bought my ticket last month. I _____ visit Paris from July 1 to July 14.

5. A: This box is too heavy!
   B: Wait! I _____ help you.

C   Read what these new students are planning to do. Make sentences using *be (not) going to* with a partner.

Carlos

Ariana

Max and Sara

☐ live at home

☐ apply for scholarships

☐ study business

☐ major in law

☐ live in the dorms

☐ go to a large university

☐ live in student housing

☐ study together

☐ work part-time

Carlos is going to live at home. He's not going to apply for scholarships.

ASK ANSWER

What about you? What are your future plans for school or work?

7 Communication Find someone who . . .

A The two questions in the chart ask about someone's future plans. Read the answers. Then complete each question with *be going to*. Check answers with a partner.

yes / no questions	_____ **study** English this summer?	Yes, I am. / Maybe. / No, I'm not.
wh- questions	What _____ **do** after graduation?	I'm going to take a trip.

B Read the questions on the left side of the chart. In the "Me" column, check (✔) the activities you're planning to do in the future. Then add your own question.

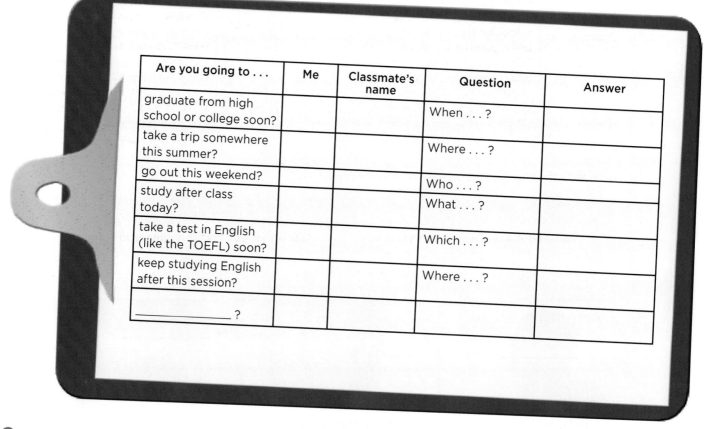

Are you going to . . .	Me	Classmate's name	Question	Answer
graduate from high school or college soon?			When . . . ?	
take a trip somewhere this summer?			Where . . . ?	
go out this weekend?			Who . . . ?	
study after class today?			What . . . ?	
take a test in English (like the TOEFL) soon?			Which . . . ?	
keep studying English after this session?			Where . . . ?	
_____ ?				

C Interview your classmates. For each question, find a different person who answers *yes*. Write the classmate's name. Ask another question to get more details.

Yes, I am.

Next month.

Are you going to graduate from college soon?

When are you going to graduate?

D Look at the answers you got in **C**. Which one was the most interesting? Tell the class.

Student Life

1   Vocabulary Link   One of these days . . .

A   Read about these two people. Then answer the questions with a partner.

1. What is each person planning to do in the future? When is he or she planning to do it?
2. Which person has more of a definite plan about his or her future?

I'm going to graduate the day after tomorrow. I'm finishing school, but I've already got lots of plans for the future. This summer, for example, I'm going to study for the medical school exam. Next year, I hope to enter medical school, and someday, I plan to be a doctor.

Carmen

I'm going to graduate in two weeks. I'm a little nervous because after graduation, I don't have any clear plans. I'd like to take a short vacation in the near future—maybe next month. Sooner or later, I also need to get a job, but I don't know what I want to do exactly. I'm sure I'll make a decision—one of these days.

Gabe

B   Complete the chart with the blue time expressions in **A**.

Future Time Expressions	
Talk about a definite (specific) time	**Talk about an indefinite (uncertain) time**
tomorrow	soon
the _____	in a few days
in two hours / days / _____ / months / years	in the_____
next week / _____ / _____	_____
this _____ / spring / fall / winter	someday / one _____
_____ graduation / school / work	

C   Complete the sentences. Then check your answers with a partner.

1. If today is Thursday, *the day after tomorrow* is _____.
2. It's 2:00. You say, "I'll be home *in two hours*." You'll be home at _____:00.
3. It's May. You say, "I'm going to graduate *next June*." This means you're going to graduate next month / in 13 months.
4. It's May. You say, "I'm going to graduate *this June*." This means you're going to graduate next month / in 13 months.
5. Your friend says, "We should have coffee *one of these days*." He or She is / isn't making an appointment with you.
6. If you tell a friend, "I'm going to Jamaica *in a few days*," you are / aren't going to Jamaica very soon.

D   Are you going to do any of these things in the future? When? Tell a partner.

complete this English class   have children   take a trip somewhere   see my friends

2 Listening   Career Day

A   Look at the photos. What are the people doing? How do you prepare for these activities?

a written exam

a physical exam

CD 1
Track 39

B   You're going to hear an ad for Career Day. Read the questions. Then listen and check the correct answers.

1. Who is Career Day for?   ☐ students   ☐ teachers   ☐ parents

2. What is another word for *career*?   ☐ school   ☐ child   ☐ job

CD 1
Track 40

C   Listen to Jeff, a speaker at Career Day, describe a process. Put the steps in order from 1 to 5.
Then complete the sentence.

_____ take a written exam   _____ take final exams   _____ go to school for four months

_____ take training courses   _____ take a physical exam

Jeff is going to be a _____.

> **ASK   ANSWER**
>
> Jeff completed all the steps in **C**. Which step would be the hardest for you? Why?

3 Reading   An opportunity of a lifetime

A   The people below are talking about Stephanie. Read what they say.
What do you think Stephanie is going to do this summer? Share with a partner.

Mrs. Lee, mother

> She's going to travel alone for six months. It's a great opportunity!

Mr. Lee, father

> After she finishes her work assignment, I'm going to meet her in Europe.

> This is a perfect job for her. She loves to take photos and meet new people.

Tommy Farr, boyfriend

B   Now read the web page. Was your guess about Stephanie's summer plans correct?

NEWS	UPDATE	PHOTOS	CONTACT US

We now have a winner! Stephanie Lee from Vancouver, Canada, answered our questions and won the top prize: she's going to be our youth travel reporter in Europe! A week after college graduation, Stephanie starts her six-month travel adventure. She'll write about her experiences for our World Link website. Here were some of Stephanie's answers to our questions:

Do you have any international travel experience and what does this tell us about you?
Yes, I do. Two years ago, I spent the summer in Hong Kong. I stayed with my grandmother and worked in the family business. I also visited Africa last year. I think this shows that I'm self-sufficient—I can do things on my own—and that I'm not afraid of new experiences.

In Africa, I went to Tanzania. The highlight was climbing Mount Kilimanjaro. It's the highest mountain in Africa. The climb was very hard. Two people turned back before they reached the top. I made it all the way! Once I start something, I never give up.

What do you think will be the hardest part of this job?
I'm going to be visiting over 25 countries where people speak lots of different languages so communicating with others might be difficult sometimes. I speak some French and German, and English, of course. I'll also be traveling with a translator in many places so I'm sure that will help. I'm also sure that sooner or later, I'm going to miss my family and friends. It's normal. But I also know from experience that this feeling will pass—especially when you meet new people.

Why should we choose you?
Because I love to travel and meet new people. I'm also a hard worker and will have no trouble filing reports on time. I'm always very punctual!

Stephanie

C Find a word or phrase in the text that has the same meaning as the words below.

1. independent _____

2. quit _____

3. speaking _____

4. lively, with a lot of energy _____

D Complete the sentences about Stephanie's new job with words from the box.
(You will not use all the words.)

Africa	punctual	school	reporter	translator
photographing	Europe	popular	talking to	website

1. Stephanie Lee is going to spend her summer in _____.

2. She's going to work as a _____ for a _____.

3. The hardest part of the job will probably be _____ new people.

4. Stephanie is perfect for the job because she's very _____.

ASK ANSWER

1. Look at answer 4 in **D**. What other reasons is Stephanie perfect for the job?

2. Would you like to do Stephanie's job? Why or why not?

4 Language Link   Predictions with *be going to* and *will*

A People use *be going to* and *will* to make predictions (guesses about the future). Look at the pictures and read the captions. Then complete sentences 1 and 2 with *be going to* or *will*.

A I'm sure you're going to be very successful.
or
I'm sure you'll be very successful.

B "Look! That truck is going to go through that red light!"

> 1. In picture A, the man is making a general prediction about the student's future, so he can use _____ or _____.
>
> 2. In picture B, we can see that the action is happening now or very soon, so we use _____ but not _____.

B The sentences below all make predictions. Complete each with *be going to, will,* or both. Then explain your answer choices to a partner.

1. Liam did really well in college. I'm sure he _____ get a good job.

2. I think you _____ like this movie. It's a comedy and you like funny movies.

3. The score is 5 to 1 and there's only one minute left in the game. Our team _____ lose for sure.

4. Scientists now believe there _____ be nine billion people on Earth by the year 2040.

5. Look at those dark clouds. It _____ rain soon.

C Study the information in the chart. Then read the predictions below. Do you think each one will happen? Why or why not? Tell a partner.

Making predictions about the future		
Leo studied hard.	**I'm sure / I bet**	he's going to / he'll <u>pass</u> the test.
Mona didn't study.		she isn't going to / she won't <u>pass</u> the test.

- It's common to use *I'm sure* and *I bet* to make a prediction you are certain about.
- Use *probably* or *maybe* when you aren't 100% sure about your prediction:
    He'll <u>probably</u> pass the test.
    She <u>probably</u> won't pass the test.
    <u>Maybe</u> we'll find a cure for cancer someday.

1. We'll find life on other planets.

2. Scientists will cure diseases like AIDS and cancer.

3. Newspapers and magazines will disappear. All information will be online.

> In the near future, we'll probably find life on other planets . . .

> Really? Maybe it'll happen, but not in the near future . . .

5 Writing — My life now and in the future

A Use the topics below or ones of your own. First, write about what you are doing now. Then write about your future. Use *be going to* and *will* to make predictions.

> family   job   travel   school   love life

My Life Now and in the Future

Right now, I'm taking an English class.

I'm working part-time at a cafe.

I live at home with my parents and two brothers. I have a boyfriend.

Someday, I'm going to get married and live in a house by the ocean. Sooner or later, I'll . . .

B Exchange papers with a partner. Do you think your partner's predictions will come true?

6 Communication — Predicting the future

A Read this profile of Prince William. With a partner, make some predictions about his future.

Birthday: June 21, 1982

Schooling: He attended university at St. Andrews in Scotland. He studied art history. After graduation, he also lived and worked for a short time in Chile, Belize, and parts of Africa. He is now a pilot with the Royal Air Force.

Hobbies: He loves sports, including rugby, hockey, swimming, skiing, and running. He likes to listen to music.

Personality: He is shy in public. In private, he is strong-willed and independent.

> Someday, he's probably going to be the King of England.

> I bet he'll marry someone famous, too, like a movie star.

B Now complete your own personal profile.

Schooling:

Hobbies:

Personality:

C Exchange profiles with a partner. Make predictions about your partner's job, travel, school, family, and love life.

> I think you're going to get a good job someday. And you'll probably also . . .

Check out the World Link video.

Practice your English online at http://elt.heinle.com/worldlink

Review: Units 4-6

1 Storyboard

A Ruben is talking to his teacher, Gina Walker. Complete the conversations.
Then tell a partner: Why does Ruben want to talk to Professor Walker?

Hello? This is Gina Walker.

Professor Walker? Hi, it's Ruben Vega. I'm calling because I'd _____ to make an _____ to see you this week.

Sure, Ruben. I have office hours _____ afternoon from 3:30 to 4:30.

today

3:30 – 4:30 Office Hours

Yeah, I know, but that time _____ for me. I have class then.

OK, _____ tomorrow at 4:30 instead?

4:30

Sure, that _____.

Later in Ms. Walker's office . . .

So, how can I help you today, Ruben?

Application

Well, I'm _____ to different business schools in London.

OK . . .

And I need a recommendation from a teacher . . .

So, would _____ writing a recommendation for me?

No. _____. You're an excellent student, Ruben!

B Practice the conversation with a partner.
Then change roles and practice again.

2 See It and Say It

A Look at the neighborhood and discuss the questions with a partner.

- What household chores and errands can you see people doing?

- What are other people in the picture doing?

- Do you think this neighborhood is a good place to live? Why or why not?

- Is this neighborhood similar to or different from yours? Explain your answer.

B Do the following:

Student A: Where is a good place for people to meet or relax in your neighborhood? Tell your partner.

Student B: Imagine you want to go to this place. Ask your partner to . . .

- give you directions from school.

- tell you how long it takes to get there.

C Switch roles and do **B** again.

> How can I get to Bix's Cafe from here?

> Take Bus 211 to . . .

3 I Need Your Advice!

A Read sentences 1-6. What advice would you give to someone who made these statements? Think about your answers.

1. I'm always running late.

2. I forgot to bring today's English homework and it's 25% of the class grade.

3. My parents don't like my friends.

4. I have a terrible commute. It takes over two hours every day.

5. I get really nervous when I have to talk to others in English.

6. I bought a new cell phone and it's not working.

B Get into a group of three people. Write the numbers 1 to 6 on six small pieces of paper. Put the numbers in a bag or hat.

• When it's your turn, choose a number. Read aloud the problem in **A** that goes with your number. Explain the problem in more detail.

• Your partners will listen and give you advice.

• Think about their suggestions. Which person gave you the best advice? Why?

4 *Be going to* or *Will*?

A The chart shows the different uses of *be going to* and *will*. Complete the sentences below with *be going to*, *will*, or both.

	to talk about plans you already made	to talk about a sudden decision	to talk about an action that is about to happen	to make a general prediction about the future
be going to	✓		✓	✓
will		✓		✓

1. I decided to take the TOEFL exam. I _____ take it next spring.

2. It's a beautiful evening. I think I _____ take a walk.

3. The score is 10 to 1 and there's a minute left in the game. Our team _____ lose for sure.

4. I bet there _____ be thousands of people at the free concert in the park tomorrow.

5. What _____ do this weekend? Do you have any plans?

6. A: The two o'clock movie is sold out, but we still have seats for the four o'clock show.
   B: OK, I _____ take two tickets for the 4:00 show.

7. Hurry! Class starts in two minutes. We _____ be late!

8. She's really smart. I bet she _____ get accepted to a good school.

B Compare your answers with a partner's. Explain why you chose *be going to*, *will*, or both in **A**.

5 Listening

A Read the poll below and choose your answer. Then take a class vote.
What was the most common answer in your class?

POLL:
Do you think you'll get married?
a. Yes, definitely. I want to get married.
b. Yes, maybe someday, but I'm not sure when.
c. No, never. Marriage isn't for me.

CD 1
Track 41

B A magazine asked a group of university students for their opinions on different topics.
Listen and put the charts in the order (1-4) you hear them talked about.

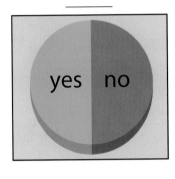

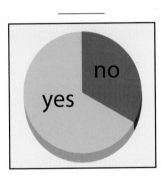

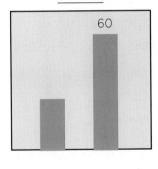

CD 1
Track 41

C Listen again and label the parts of each chart in **B** with the correct numbers / percentages.
Some numbers will not be given. You have to guess them.

D Look at your answers (1-4) in **B**. What do the students interviewed think?
Read the sentences below and then choose the correct answer.

Chart 1: Most / Some of the students think it's OK for couples with children to get divorced.

Chart 2: This year, a couple / more of them think studying abroad is good.

Chart 3: Most / Half of them think the university entrance exam is too difficult.

Chart 4: A lot / Almost none of them think plastic surgery is OK.

> ⓘ **plastic surgery:** a medical operation that changes or improves your looks

E What do you think about the four opinions in **D**?
Compare your ideas with a partner's. Explain your reasons.

> I think it's OK for couples with kids to get divorced.

> Sorry, but I don't agree . . .

7 Let's Celebrate

Lesson A   Party time!

1   Vocabulary Link   Different kinds of parties

A   Look at the photos of the different parties. Then take the quiz below. Circle the correct words.

a 21st birthday party

a rave

a housewarming party

a bachelor party

a Super Bowl party

a baby shower

American Party Quiz

1. When you turn 21, your friends may have a party for you. Everyone celebrates you *getting your first job / becoming an adult*.

2. A rave is an all-night party. Lots of people get together to dance and have a good time. It's usually outdoors or in a large building. It's often pretty *quiet / wild*.

3. When people get a new house or apartment, sometimes they throw a housewarming party. If you're invited to this type of party, bring the host *a gift / some money* for his or her new house.

4. Before the wedding, a *man's / woman's* friends may plan a bachelor party for *him / her*. It's often a rowdy celebration of the person's last "free" days before marriage.

5. Every February, two American football teams compete in a big sporting event called the Super Bowl. Many people get together at friends' houses to eat, drink, and root for their favorite *team / player*.

6. You have a baby shower for a pregnant woman *before / after* her baby is born. A close female friend or relative hosts the party and the woman gets presents for the child.

rowdy is a party breaking the rules

 B   With a partner, check your answers on page 154. Then discuss these questions.

> *i* What two phrases in **A** mean the same thing as *have a party*?

1. In your country, are there parties like the ones in the United States? How are they similar to or different from the American ones?

2. When was the last time you went to a party?

   • What kind of party was it?

   • How many people were invited?

   • Who threw it?

   • Did you have a good time?

2 Listening — An important day

CD 2
Track 2

A Two speakers are going to talk about an important celebration in their countries. Read sentences 1 and 2. Then listen and complete them.

1. Both speakers are talking about a type of _____ celebration.
   a. birthday   b. graduation   c. pre-wedding

2. In both countries, this celebration is important because it's when a person
   _____.

CD 2
Track 3

B Read sentences a–l below. Then listen and match a celebration with the correct answers. Some answers are true for both celebrations.

The Rose Party: _____

a. You are 20.

b. You are 15.

c. It happens in Japan.

d. It happens in El Salvador.

e. It's only for young women.

f. You wear special clothes.

Coming of Age Day: _____

g. Everyone celebrates together on a day in January.

h. There's a ceremony at City Hall first.

i. There's a religious ceremony first.

j. You get gifts.

k. Many people come to your home to eat and dance.

l. You go with friends to different clubs and parties.

C Choose one celebration from above. Use your answers in **A** and **B** and describe it to a partner.

> **ASK** **ANSWER**
> Is there a similar celebration in your country? When is it and what happens?

3 Pronunciation — Reduced *want to*

> **ⓘ** In spoken English, *want to* is often pronounced *wanna*.

CD 2
Track 4

A Listen and notice the pronunciation of *want to* in the sentences and questions.

1. Do you <u>want to</u> have coffee after class?

2. We <u>want to</u> have a party on Saturday.

3. Do you <u>want to</u> get together this weekend?

4. My parents <u>want to</u> invite you to dinner.

CD 2
Track 5

B Listen and complete the dialog. Then practice it with a partner.

A: _____ do this weekend?

B: I'm not sure. Oh, wait . . . I know. _____ see that new sci-fi movie. _____ come with me?

A: I don't really _____ see that movie.

B: OK. What _____ do?

4 Speaking   **Do you want to go with me?**

CD 2
Track 6

A Listen to the conversation. Then answer the questions with a partner.

1. Omar is going to a party. What kind of party is it? How does Omar invite Lane?

2. Does Lane accept? What does she say?

Omar: Hey, Lane. My classmate Sayuri is having a party this weekend.

Lane: Really?

Omar: Yeah, it's a costume party.

Lane: Sounds like fun.

Omar: Do you want to go with me?

Lane: Are you sure? I don't really know Sayuri.

Omar: No problem. She said I could invite a friend.

Lane: OK, then. I'd love to go. When exactly is it?

Omar: On Saturday night.

Lane: Wow, that's the day after tomorrow! I need to get a costume.

Omar: Me, too. There's a good place near here that rents them. Let's go there after school.

Lane: Sounds good!

B Practice the conversation with a partner.

5 Speaking Strategy

A Use the Useful Expressions and the words in the box below to form invitations.

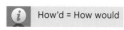 How'd = How would

Useful Expressions		
Inviting someone to do something		**Accepting or refusing an invitation**
Do you want **Would you like** **How'd you like**	to go with me?	Sure, I'd love to. That sounds great. I'm sorry, but I can't. I have plans. Unfortunately, I can't. I have to work. I'd love to, but I'm busy.

study for our English test	see a movie	after class	tomorrow
come to my birthday party	your idea:_____	this weekend	tonight

1. How'd you like to study for our English test after class?

2. _____

3. _____

4. _____

B Take turns inviting your partner to the events in **A**. Refuse two of your partner's invitations. Give an excuse (a reason for saying "no").

> We have an English test this Friday. How'd you like to study for it after class?

> I'd love to but . . .

6 Language Link   Similarity and agreement with *so, too, either, neither*

A Study the information in the chart. Then match each of student A's statements below with the correct response. Check your answers with a partner.

	Affirmative Answers	Negative Answers
with *be*	I <u>am</u> going to Sayuri's party. So am I. / I am, too. / Me, too.	I'<u>m not</u> going to Sayuri's party. Neither am I. / I'm not, either. / Me, neither.
other verbs	I <u>need</u> a costume for the party. So do I. / I do, too. / Me, too.	I <u>don't have</u> a costume for the party. Neither do I. / I don't, either. / Me, neither.

Student A says . . .

1. I'm having a party this weekend.
2. Tim and Monica speak Spanish.
3. I missed the bus this morning.
4. I was late for my first class.
5. The teacher wasn't here yesterday.
6. I didn't have a good time at that party.

Student B responds . . .

Neither was I.

Neither did I.

So do I.

So did I.

I was, too.

So am I.

> ℹ️ *Me, too* and *me, neither* are common in casual conversation.

B Agree with each statement in at least two ways.

1. I like to go to parties.

   _____

2. I'm never late to class.

   _____

3. I don't speak Italian.

   _____

4. I'm planning to study abroad next year.

   _____

5. I think I did well on the exam.

   _____

C Complete the statements below with information about yourself.

1. I like to _____ on the weekend.

2. I don't like to _____ during class.

3. I need to _____ before I graduate.

4. I think _____ parties are fun.

D Compare your opinions in **C** with a partner. Then switch roles and do the exercise again.

> I like to go out with my friends on the weekend.

> So do I. Where do you usually go?

> Not me. I like to hang out and relax at home.

7 Communication   Party planning

A Plan a party with a partner. Choose an item from each category or think of an item of your own.

Type of party

a. a costume party   b. a pool party   c. a birthday party

Place

a. a friend's house   b. a nightclub   c. a park

Type of food

a. finger foods   b. barbecue   c. pasta and salad

B Invite four other pairs to your party. Ask and answer questions about their parties. Complete the invitations below.

> Would you like to come to our party next week?

> What kind of party is it?

> It's a surprise birthday party for Antonio. He turns 22 next Friday.

Type of party: _____
Place: _____
Food: _____

Type of party: _____
Place: _____
Food: _____

Type of party: _____
Place: _____
Food: _____

Type of party: _____
Place: _____
Food: _____

C Discuss the parties in **B** with your partner. What do you think of each one? Choose your favorite together and then share your choice with the class.

> I really like the surprise birthday party.

> So do I. But the costume party sounds fun too.

Let's Celebrate

Lesson B Festivals and holidays

1 Vocabulary Link   International festivals

A Read about the three festivals. Then match a word or phrase in blue with the correct definition below.

International Festivals: Where do you want to go?

Carnival *(Trinidad)*

One of the largest Carnival celebrations in the world takes place in Trinidad in mid-February or early March every year. The streets of Port of Spain (the capital) are full of thousands of people watching colorful parades and dancing to music. People also compete in contests to win first prize for best costume or musical performance.

The International Festival of the Sahara *(Tunisia)*

For four days at the end of December, thousands of people gather together in Douz, a village near the Sahara Desert, to celebrate the traditions of the desert people. There are horse and camel races, and dancing and musical performances.

The Rainforest World Music Festival *(Malaysia)*

In early July, musicians from many different countries participate in this three-day "world music" event. Many afternoon performances are held in small village houses. In the evening, artists usually perform on large outdoor stages.

1. happens _____*is held*_____ , _____
2. a competition _____
3. a competition in which one tries to be the fastest _____
4. filled, having a lot of something _____
5. to sing, dance, act, or play music in front of people _____
6. to do the best in a competition _____
7. to come together in a group _____
8. something given to the winner _____
9. to join in an activity _____

Complete the chart.

Noun	Verb	Person (noun)
participation		participant
		performer
win		winner

B Get into a group of three people. Each person chooses <u>one</u> festival from **A**. Use your own words to tell your group about it by answering these questions:

ASK ANSWER

Which festival in **A** would you like to go to? Why?

- What's the festival called?
- Where and when does it happen?
- What happens at the festival?

2 Listening   The Race of Hope

A   Read the sentences below. Then listen to a news report.
Choose the best answer for each item.

1. The main topic of the news report is ___.

   a. Cameroon   b. a prize
   c. a race   d. a performance

2. This year, the woman, Nichelle, is a ___.

   a. reporter   b. winner
   c. watcher   d. participant

3. She's from ___.

   a. Cameroon   b. Kenya
   c. Ethiopia   d. the U.S.

a volcano

Mt. Cameroon

B   Listen again and complete the notes.

1. Where the event is held: _____

2. When it takes place: In _____

3. What people do: run up a _____ and then back down

4. Distance: _____ km

5. Number of participants: _____

6. To date, country all winners are from: _____

7. Prize: _____

8. Other events: During the weekend, there's also a _____.

C   Why do you think this event is called "The Race of Hope"? Listen to part of the interview again.
Then tell a partner your ideas.

3 Reading   Get ready to get dirty

A   You are going to read about two festivals. Look at the title of the reading and the photos on
the next page. Answer the questions. Then read the article and check your answers.

1. What's happening in the photos?

2. What kind of festivals do you think they are?

B   What does each festival item symbolize? Match an item with its meaning. Two answers are extra.

Festival item	symbolize(s) . . .
the oranges	the end of all bad things
the red hat	a beautiful woman
the large fire	the rocks people originally used
the colored powder	an evil man
	you don't want to fight
	a new beginning

C Circle the festival each sentence describes. In some cases, both answers are possible.

1. It's celebrated in different countries.   Orange Festival   Holi
2. It's based on an old story.   Orange Festival   Holi
3. It's a celebration of good over bad.   Orange Festival   Holi
4. You throw things at other people.   Orange Festival   Holi
5. You need to join a team to participate.   Orange Festival   Holi
6. People wear costumes.   Orange Festival   Holi

GET READY TO GET DIRTY

It's a cool February afternoon in the small town of Ivrea in Northern Italy. The streets are usually quiet, but today they're full of people as the four-day Orange Festival begins. The "Carnevale di Ivrea" is over 900 years old. It celebrates the story of a young girl named Violetta. She killed the town's evil[1] leader and set the people of Ivrea free. Today's festival remembers the fight that took place between the people of Ivrea and the evil leader's guards.[2] In the original fight, people threw beans or rocks at the soldiers. Today, participants wear colorful costumes and throw oranges instead.

The Orange Festival begins with a parade from City Hall to the center of town. A young woman dressed as Violetta speaks to the crowd and throws candy to the people. After that, the orange fights begin. Men, women, and children will run throughout the town and throw oranges at each other.

To participate in the orange-throwing contests, you need to join a team— you can be on a team that fights for freedom or you can be one of the evil leader's soldiers. If you don't want to join the fighting, you must wear a red hat (red hats are sold everywhere during the festival). Then no one will throw oranges at you. Put it on, watch out, and have fun!

[1] **evil**: very bad   [2] **guard**: a protector (e.g., a soldier or police officer)

The Festival of Color, also known as Holi, is a popular spring celebration. It takes place every year in late February or early March in India and many other countries, including Nepal and Sri Lanka. In Indian mythology,[3] an evil woman tried to kill a young man named Prahlad by burning him in a fire. Because Prahlad was a good person, he escaped from the fire unhurt. Today, people remember this event by lighting large fires in the streets on the night before Holi. The fire is a symbol of burning all things evil. The next day, Holi, is a new beginning. To celebrate, people gather in the streets. They throw colored powder into the air and shout "Holi Hai!" Others throw brightly colored water or powder on each other. By the end of the festival, the streets are filled with color and smiles!

[3] **mythology**: a collection of very old, traditional stories

D Choose a festival from the reading and explain it to a partner in your own words.

4 Language Link   Time clauses with *before*, *after*, and *when*

A Study the sentences in the chart. Notice the two ways of writing each sentence.

1a. <u>Before</u> the festival starts, you rent a costume. b. You rent a costume <u>before</u> the festival starts.	Both sentences tell us that first you rent a costume, and then the festival starts.
2a. <u>After</u> Violetta speaks to the crowd, the fights begin. b. The fights begin <u>after</u> Violetta speaks to the crowd.	Both sentences tell us that first the woman speaks, and then the fights begin.
3a. <u>When</u> people throw the powder into the air, they shout "Holi Hai!" b. People shout "Holi Hai!" <u>when</u> they throw powder into the air.	Both sentences tell us that people shout "Holi Hai!" at about the same time they throw powder into the air.

B Match a clause on the left with one on the right to make sentences about a typical day. Use each answer only once.

<u> b </u> 1. After I eat breakfast,   a. I take off my shoes and relax.

_____ 2. Before I leave the house,   b. I brush my teeth.

_____ 3. I check my e-mail   c. I say "goodbye" to my cat.

_____ 4. I have lunch   d. after I work all morning.

_____ 5. I make my last phone calls   e. after I turn on my computer.

_____ 6. When I get home from school,   f. before I leave the office.

C Read about Paloma's Three Kings Day activities. Then with a partner, combine the different sentences using *before*, *after*, and *when*.

> **January 5**
>
> 9:00 p.m. Paloma and her family go to the Three Kings Parade.
>
> **January 6**
>
> 7:00 a.m. Paloma's younger brothers get up.
> 7:00 a.m. They wake Paloma up.
> 7:15 a.m. The family gathers in the living room.
> 7:20 a.m. They open presents.
> 8:00 a.m. Everyone relaxes and enjoys the morning.
> 11:00 a.m. Paloma and her mom prepare lunch.
>
> 2:00 p.m. Paloma's grandparents arrive at her house. Everyone has lunch.
> 3:00 p.m. The family eats a special cake called a *Roscón*.
> 3:30 p.m. The adults talk and the children play games.
> 10:55 p.m. Paloma kisses her parents good night.
> 11:00 p.m. Paloma goes to bed.

> Paloma's brothers wake her up after they get up.

5 Writing   **In my country**

A   Read the paragraphs on the right. Then tell a partner:

1. Is the person writing about a festival or holiday?

2. What is it called?

3. Where and when does it happen?

4. What do people do?

B   What is a famous festival in your city or country? Use the questions in **A** to write a paragraph or two about it.

C   Exchange papers with a partner. Ask your partner one question about his or her festival.

In Korea, we have a holiday called Chusok. It usually takes place in September. It is a holiday for giving thanks and honoring ancestors.

Many people travel home to spend Chusok with their families. After they arrive home, people eat special rice cakes called songphyun. Then everyone goes to the cemetery. When they visit the cemetery, they offer rice and fruit to their ancestors.

6 Communication   **An unusual holiday**

A   Look at these unusual holidays. Then ask and answer the questions below with a partner.

World Tourism Day
September 27

National Ice Cream Day
July 20

National Men Make Dinner Day
November 7

1. What do you think happens on each day?

2. Which one(s) would you like to celebrate? Why?

B   Use the questions to invent an unusual holiday.

- What is the name of the holiday?
- What is the date of the holiday?
- What is the reason for the holiday?
- Who celebrates it?

- What do people do on the holiday?
- Do people celebrate it at home or outside the home?
- What do people wear?
- Are there any special foods or decorations?

C   Present your holiday to the class. Which is the most interesting?

 Check out the World Link video.   Practice your English online at http://elt.heinle.com/worldlink

1 Vocabulary Link   I love that show!

A The people below are talking about TV shows. Read their opinions. Then discuss the questions with a partner.

   1. What kind of show is each person talking about?   2. Does the person like the show? Why or why not?

My friend watches this nighttime soap opera called *The Good Girls*. The show tells the story of a group of teenagers in Hong Kong. They go to an elite high school. Anyway, the show is so predictable—always the same old story. A boy and girl fall in love. Then they fight. And, finally, there's a happy ending: they get back together. I think the show is boring, but my friend loves it.

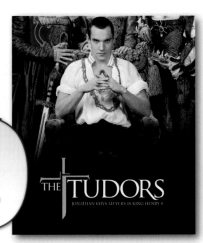

I'm totally hooked on a *TV* series called *The Tudors*—I never miss it! It's based on a true story about King Henry VIII of England and his family. Some stuff in the show is made up, but usually, the story is very realistic—it's based on actual events. The characters are great (especially King Henry) and the stories are really interesting. But you have to watch every episode or the story is hard to follow.

B Complete the sentences with a blue word or phrase from **A**.

1. I'm _____ the *Harry Potter* books. I can't stop reading them.

2. Everything about this movie is so _____. You can guess what happens next.

3. This painting of you is very _____. It's like a photograph!

4. A lot of the stories about her childhood are _____. Most of them aren't true.

5. Sorry, but I don't _____ you. Can you explain what you mean?

6. The story has a _____. The poor boy gets rich and marries his girlfriend.

C Think of a popular TV drama. Tell a partner about it.

- Who are the main characters?
- What's the show about?
- Are the show and characters realistic?
- Do you have to watch every episode to follow the story?
- Do you like the show? Why or why not?

2 Listening   One sentence at a time

A Read the sentences below. Then listen to an interview with writer Roberto Gonzalez. Circle *True* or *False*. Then explain your answers to a partner.

CD 2
Track 9

1. Roberto writes love stories.   True   False

2. Many of his stories are based on real people and events.   True   False

3. His newest story has a happy ending.   True   False

4. One of his stories will be made into a movie.   True   False

5. These days, Roberto is writing a story about a Japanese cell phone. True   False

B Roberto is working on a new story. Read the sentences below.
Then listen to the rest of the interview and circle the correct answers.

CD 2
Track 10

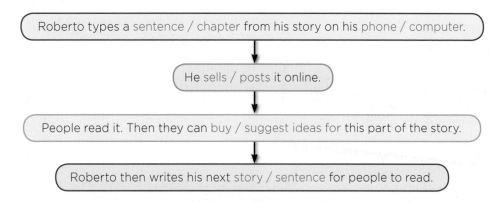

Roberto types a sentence / chapter from his story on his phone / computer.

↓

He sells / posts it online.

↓

People read it. Then they can buy / suggest ideas for this part of the story.

↓

Roberto then writes his next story / sentence for people to read.

C Listen again and check your answers in **B**. Then answer the questions with a partner.

CD 2
Track 10

1. How is Roberto writing his new story?

2. How do his readers help him?

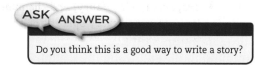

ASK ANSWER

Do you think this is a good way to write a story?

3 Pronunciation   *Was* vs. *wasn't*; *were* vs. *weren't*

A Listen and check (✔) the sentence you hear.

CD 2
Track 11

1. ☐ He was reading a story.   ☐ He wasn't reading a story.

2. ☐ She was walking to work.   ☐ She wasn't walking to work.

3. ☐ They were working hard.   ☐ They weren't working hard.

4. ☐ They were having fun.   ☐ They weren't having fun.

B Read the sentences in **A** aloud. Practice with a partner.

UNIT 8 • Storytelling   81

4 Speaking   So then what happened?

A Mia is telling Nico a story. Listen and then answer the questions with a partner.

CD 2
Track 12

1. Who is the story about?   2. Where is he from?   3. What happened to him?

Mia: Hey, Nico, listen to this story. It's like something from a fairy tale.

Nico: Yeah? What's it about?

Mia: It's about this guy from Uganda. He came to the U.S. as a student.

Nico: Yeah?

Mia: Yeah, but then things got really difficult in his country and he couldn't go back. So, he stayed in the U.S. He got two jobs, but he was still poor.

Nico: Sounds like a hard life.

Mia: Yeah, but then a month ago, he finally returned to his country. It turns out he was really a prince!

Nico: Wait . . . he was living in the U.S. and he was really poor, but he was a *prince*?

Mia: Yeah!

Nico: So, then what happened?

Mia: Well, in the end, he stayed in Uganda and became king of his tribe¹.

Nico: Wow, what a great story!

¹ **tribe**: group of related families who live in the same area

B Practice the conversation with a partner.

5 Speaking Strategy

A On a separate piece of paper, write a word or single sentence for the following:

1. a person's name
2. another person's name
3. a place
4. how the two people met
5. what happened to the two people

Useful Expressions: Telling a story		
Introducing the story	**Continuing the story**	**Ending the story**
It's (a story) about . . .	So (then), . . .	In the end, . . .
The story begins / starts in . . .	Later . . .	Finally, . . .
One day . . .	After that, . . .	
	It turns out that . . .	

B Exchange papers with a partner. Use your partner's notes and the Useful Expressions to make up a story.

ⓘ **Asking about a story**

What's it about?
So then what happened?
Really? / Yeah?

C Get together with a new partner and do the following:

Student A: Tell your story.

Student B: Listen. Then tell your partner: What did you like about the story?

D Switch roles and do **C** again.

What's your story about?

It's about a high school student named Jonah. One day on the subway, he found a wallet full of money . . .

6 Language Link   Past continuous vs. simple past

A Look at the pictures and read the sentences. Then answer the questions below with a partner.

Tom was walking down the street.

Suddenly, he stopped and turned around.

Someone was following him.

Which verbs describe . . .

- an action in progress at a certain time in the past? Circle them.
- a completed or finished action in the past? Underline them.

B Maya and Sami are talking about a TV show. Complete the dialog with the simple past or the past continuous of the verbs in parentheses.

The past continuous		
I / He / She	was walking	down the street.
You / We / They	were walking	

Sami: Hey, Maya. I (1. try) _____ to call you last night. Where (2. be) _____ you?

Maya: I (3. watch) _____ that show *Lonely Hearts*. I guess I (4. not hear) _____ my phone.

Sami: Oh, I love that show! I (5. miss) _____ last night's episode. What (6. happen) _____ ?

Maya: Well, in the opening scene, Stefano (7. talk) _____ on the phone to Nicole.

> ℹ Don't use stative verbs (*be, have, need, know*, etc.) with the past continuous. Use the simple past.

Sami: Wait . . . Nicole is Stefano's girlfriend, right?

Maya: Yeah, remember? Nicole and Stefano (8. be) _____ together in Sydney.

Sami: In Sydney? What (9. do) _____ Stefano _____ in Sydney?

Maya: He (10. go) _____ to college there three years ago. He (11. meet) _____ Nicole there. They (12. fall) _____ in love while they (13. work) _____ on a project together.

Sami: Oh, yeah . . . now I remember. But then Stefano (14. have) _____ to return to Italy because his father (15. die) _____ suddenly.

Maya: Right. Then later, Stefano (16. get) _____ a job in Rome. But he never (17. forget) _____ about Nicole.

C Check your answers in **B** with a partner. Then practice the conversation together.

D Take turns asking and answering the questions with a partner.

1. What were you doing last night at 8:00?
2. What were you wearing two days ago?
3. What were you studying in last Monday's class?
4. Who were you sitting next to in class yesterday?

7 Communication   Who's telling the truth?

CD 2
Track 13

A Both Jenna and Ryan say they were in a car accident. One person is lying.
Listen to each person's story and take some notes below.

	Jenna	Ryan
When did it happen?		
Where did it happen?		
What happened?		
What color was the car?		
Who was driving?		

B In **A**, who do you think is making up a story? How do you know?
Discuss your ideas with a partner.

C Think about something funny or unusual that happened to you.
Then do the following steps with a partner:

1. **Student A:** Tell your story.
   Student B: Listen and take some notes on *who*, *what*, *where*, *when*, and *why*.

2. Change roles and repeat step 1.

3. Now choose <u>one</u> of your stories. You are both going to tell this same story to another pair.

D Get together with another pair.

- **Pair 1:** Each person should say one sentence to start your story.

- **Pair 2:** Ask each person in Pair 1 questions about their story. You have
  one minute. Then guess: who is telling the truth and who is making up
  the story? How do you know?

E Switch roles and do **D** again.

> I was on TV once.

> OK, Person 1: What were you doing on TV?

> I was on TV once.

Storytelling

Lesson B Happily ever after

1 Vocabulary Link Modern fairy tales

A Read about the two movies below. Use the definitions in the box to help you.

> **brave:** not afraid, without fear
> **clever:** smart, quick thinking
> **eventually:** finally
> **incredible:** hard to believe, amazing
>
> **overcome:** to successfully deal with a problem
> **struggle:** to try hard to do something difficult
> **survive:** to stay alive
> **uneducated:** having little or no schooling

Homeless to Harvard tells the story of 16-year-old Liz Murray. After her father leaves home and her mother dies, Liz has to live on the streets of New York City. Alone and afraid, she struggles a lot. She survives by sleeping in subways or at friends' houses. In time, this brave teen overcomes many difficulties and eventually she graduates from Harvard University.

Slumdog Millionaire tells the story of 18-year-old Jamal, a poor boy from one of Mumbai's worst neighborhoods. When Jamal starts winning money on a TV quiz show, people ask: How can an uneducated boy be so successful? Is he cheating or is he really clever? *Slumdog Millionaire* is an incredible story you'll never forget!

B Work with a partner. Choose one of the movies from **A** and answer the questions about it.

1. What's the movie about? Describe it in your own words.

2. Have you ever seen the movie? If yes, did you like it? If not, would you like to see it?

> **The prefixes *un-* and *in-***
>
> Find the words in **A** that begin with *un-* or *in-*. What do these prefixes mean?
>
> What do you think the words below mean?
>
> unpredictable   incorrect
>
> unbelievable   inexperienced

> **ASK ANSWER**
>
> Do you know a story about a person who overcame some difficulty? What did the person do?

2 Listening The moral of the story is . . .

A Which words in the box do you know? Which words do you think describe the animals in the picture? Tell a partner.

hare

tortoise

> arrogant   patient   quick   slow

CD 2
Track 14

B Marnie and her dad are talking. Read sentences 1–3. Then listen and circle the correct answer(s).

1. There's a contest / game / test at school and Marnie thinks she's going to fail / lose / win.

2. Laura Sanders is Marnie's best friend / competitor / teacher.

3. Laura is very talented / funny / kind.

CD 2
Track 15

C Marnie's dad tells her the story "The Tortoise and the Hare." Listen and write *H* for hare and *T* for tortoise.

1. The ____ challenges the ____.   4. The ____ finishes the race first.

2. The ____ thinks he will win the race.   5. The ____ was arrogant.

3. The ____ takes a rest during the race.   6. The ____ was clever.

D Listen again. Marnie's dad gives her some advice by telling the story of the tortoise and the hare. What is his advice? List your ideas in two or three sentences.

CD 2
Track 15

Marnie's dad gives her this advice: _____

_____

_____

> **ASK** ANSWER
>
> Do you agree with the father's advice?
> Why or why not?

3 Reading The Cinderella story

A Look at the title and the photos on page 87. What do you know about the fairy-tale character Cinderella? Tell a partner.

B Read the passage on page 87. Then write the headers below in the correct places in the reading. Two headers are extra.

One story, many cultures   A present-day Cinderella
Cinderella in the movies   The African Cinderella
Why we love her   A famous fairy tale

The Cinderella Story

1. _____

The Cinderella story is a famous one. Cinderella was
living happily with her family when her mother died.
Her father remarried. Cinderella's new stepmother
5 and two stepsisters treated her poorly. She had to
wear old clothes and work hard while the sisters
wore fancy clothes and had fun.

You know the rest of the story. A good fairy helped Cinderella. She turned Cinderella's old clothes into a
beautiful dress. Cinderella went to a party and a prince fell in love with her. Cinderella left the party in a
10 hurry and didn't tell the prince her name. But she did leave a glass slipper and the prince used that to find
her. Eventually, Cinderella and the Prince married and lived happily ever after.

2. _____

That's one telling of the story, but the Cinderella fairy tale is found in many different countries with minor
differences. In an African version, for example, there is one stepsister, not two. In a version from the
15 Philippines, a forest spirit helps the Cinderella character. Settareh, a Middle Eastern Cinderella, goes to a
New Year's party. And Cinderella is not always a woman. In an Irish story, a young boy, Becan, marries a
princess and lives happily ever after.

3. _____

There are also modern retellings of the Cinderella story. In one, a girl named Cindy Ella is a student at a Los
20 Angeles high school. Her fashionable stepmother and older stepsisters care a lot about shopping and money.
Cindy doesn't. When she writes a letter to her school newspaper against a school dance, she becomes very
unpopular with both students and teachers. Only her two best friends—and later the school's most
handsome boy—support her.

4. _____

25 Why is the Cinderella story so popular and found in so many cultures? There are several reasons. First
of all, it's a romantic story, which is a popular style. Also, Cinderella is a kind girl with a hard life.
That makes people want to root for her. But maybe most important is that in the Cinderella story,
a person faces many challenges but overcomes them in the end. That's a story that everyone—
boy or girl, young or old— wants to believe can come true.

C Match the names on the left with the information on the right to make true sentences.
One answer is extra.

1. The African Cinderella	a. attends a New Year's party.
2. Becan	b. has a forest spirit help her.
3. Cindy Ella	c. has only one stepsister.
4. The Philippine Cinderella	d. is a "boy" Cinderella.
5. Settareh	e. is an unpopular high school student.
	f. was a movie version of the Cinderella story.

ASK ANSWER

Why is the Cinderella story so popular? The reading lists three
reasons. Do you agree with these reasons?

Is there a Cinderella story in your country? If so, what is the story?

4 Language Link **Adverbs of manner**

A Read the sentences in the box. Notice the adverbs in blue. Then complete sentences 1–3 below.

> Cinderella danced happily with the prince.
> She ran quickly down the stairs and lost a shoe.
>
> The tortoise walked slowly across the finish line.
> The hare ran fast, but he still lost the race.

1. Adverbs of manner tell you how / why something is done.

2. Adverbs of manner usually come before / after a verb.

3. Adverbs of manner often / always end in -*ly*.

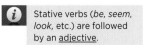 Stative verbs (*be, seem, look*, etc.) are followed by an <u>adjective</u>.

B Circle the adjective or adverb to complete Daniel Tammet's profile.

Daniel Tammet was born with a brain disorder (a type of illness). Because of it, Daniel was different / differently from other children. As a boy, he liked to play alone and acted strange / strangely around others. In school, he struggled to do good / well. To many of his classmates, Daniel seemed unusual / unusually and they laughed at him. This hurt Daniel deep / deeply, and he became very shy / shyly.

As a teenager, things changed. Daniel discovered he had an incredible ability. He could solve difficult math problems almost instant / instantly. He also discovered another talent: he could learn to speak a language very quick / quickly. Today, he is fluent / fluently in twelve languages.

As an adult, Daniel has overcome his shyness. He wrote two books and now he travels constant / constantly to talk to people about his life and his experience.

Daniel Tammet
Nickname: Brain Man
From: the UK

C Discuss the questions with a partner.

1. As a child, how did Daniel act? Why?

2. How did people treat Daniel? How did this influence him?

3. What two special abilities does Daniel have?

4. Does Daniel's story end happily? Why or why not?

D Get into a group of 3-4 people. Add two more verbs and adverbs to the chart below.

Verbs		Adverbs	
climb	sing	calmly	nervously
dance	_____	carefully	quickly
laugh	_____	gracefully	quietly
run		happily	_____
		terribly	_____

E Choose a verb and an adverb. Then act out the combination. Can your group guess what you're doing? Take turns with the people in your group.

> You're singing terribly!

5 Writing   A fairy-tale diary

A Look at the picture from the Cinderella story. Answer the questions with a partner.

- Who is in the picture?
- Where are they?
- What's happening?

B Look again at the picture and follow the instructions.

- It's the next day (the day after the party).
- Choose a character from the picure in **A**. Write a diary entry in that character's words. You can make up information.
- Write at least eight sentences in your entry. Use at least three -*ly* adverbs.

Last night, I went to a party. I met this incredibly beautiful girl there. I asked her to dance slowly with me. We were having a lot of fun, but then suddenly at midnight, she left the party very quickly . . .

6 Communication   Guess who I am

A Get into a group of three to four people and do the following:

Student A: Read your diary entry from Writing to your group. Try to act it out with feeling.

Students B, C, and D: Listen to Student A's entry. Then answer these questions:

1. Who is Student A?

2. What did you like most about his or her diary entry?

B Switch roles and repeat **A** again.

The world's oldest Cinderella story was written in 850 A.D. and comes from _____.
a. Germany
b. China
c. Iran

Check out the World Link video.   Practice your English online at http://elt.heinle.com/worldlink

9 The World of Work
Lesson A Work history

1 Vocabulary Link Job qualities

A Read about the job of a <u>paramedic.</u> Then tell a partner: could you be a paramedic? Why or why not?

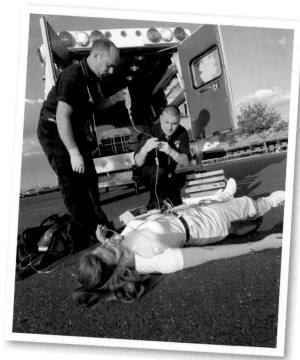

- In an emergency, paramedics are often the first to arrive. They have to be knowledgeable about different ways to help sick and injured people. They also have to be courageous in dangerous situations.

- Paramedics need to be efficient in their actions and work quickly. At the same time, they have to be cautious—especially when moving an injured person.

- Sometimes, the injured person can be rude. Whatever happens, a paramedic must stay calm and be pleasant.

- Paramedics need to be independent and able to make good decisions on their own. They also need to be punctual when coming to work. An emergency call can come at any time.

- Finally, a paramedic's job is unpredictable. Every day and every situation is different. Paramedics have to be flexible and able to deal with changes as they happen.

B Match a blue word in **A** with its definition.

1. friendly, nice to people _Pleasant_
2. knowing a lot _Knowledgeable_
3. on time _punctual_
4. careful _Cautious_
5. able to change easily _efficient_
6. able to work alone _independent_
7. brave _courageous_
8. always changing _Unpredictab_
9. organized and fast _flexible._

List other words from **B** that end in *-able / -ible*, *-ent / -ant*, or *-ous*. Which part of speech (noun, verb, adjective) are these words? Do you know other words that end in these suffixes?

-able / -ible	knowledgeable, unpredictable	adjective
-ent / -ant	independent, pleasant, efficient	adjective
-ous	courageous, cautious	adjective

C Discuss the questions with a partner.

1. What is the hardest thing about being a paramedic? _Courageous an efficient._
2. What other jobs have unpredictable schedules? Which ones require you to be courageous? pleasant? flexible? _Firefighters, Doctors, Nurses, Police officers._
3. Which words in **B** describe you? Explain.

Wellbeing = health
wellness = life styles

2 Listening   **It's hard work.**

A Look at the jobs below. What are the advantages (good things) and disadvantages (bad things) of each job? Tell your partner.

> taxi driver   flight attendant   tour guide

CD 2
Track 16

B You will hear a man talking about his job. Which job in **A** does he do? Circle it. What information helped you choose your answer? _flight attendant._

Disadvantages	Advantages
1. You're _away_ from _home_ a lot—about _twenty_ days a month. • It's hard to have a _social_ life. 2. The job is hard on your _health_ • You _stand_ a lot. _16 hours_ • It's difficult to get enough _sleep_ and to _eat_ right. 3. Sometimes, there's a _rude_ person. You have to be _friendly_ and _helpful_	1. You meet _some interesting people_ 2. You get to _visit_ lots of _Places._

CD 2
Track 16

C What are the disadvantages and advantages of this job?

1. Read the statements in the chart. Try to guess the answers.

2. Listen again and complete the statements. Use one word in each blank.

ASK ANSWER

Do you think the speaker likes his job? Why or why not?

Would you like to do this job? Why or why not?

D The man suggests certain qualities are important for his job. What are they? Circle the correct answers. Two words are extra. Explain your choices to a partner.

It's important to be . . .

punctual   (pleasant)   cautious   flexible   (patient)
agreeable

3 Pronunciation   **Reduced _for_ in time expressions**

CD 2
Track 17

A Listen to the sentences. Notice the reduced pronunciation of _for_.

1. My father has worked there for decades.   3. He hasn't been in class for a week.

2. I've lived in the same city for years.

CD 2
Track 18

B Listen to these sentences and write the time expressions you hear.

1. He's been sick _____.   3. She's taught school _____.

2. I haven't eaten _____.   4. I haven't seen him _____.

C Complete the sentences with information about yourself. Then say the sentences to a partner. Use reduced _for_.

1. I haven't been sick for _____

2. I've lived in _____Houston_ for _10 months_

3. I've studied English for _____.

> I've lived in the same house for ten years. I've studied English for three years.

4 Speaking — Tell me a little about yourself.

CD 2
Track 19

A Read the job ad. Then listen to an interview.
Is Ines the right person for the job? Why or why not?

Simon: So, Ines, tell me a little about yourself.

Ines: Well, I'm a first-year student at City University, and I'm majoring in journalism.

Simon: And you're working for your school's online newspaper, right?

Ines: Yeah. I write a blog. It focuses on pop culture, fashion, music . . . stuff like that.

Simon: How long have you worked there?

Ines: For about six months. I post an entry once a week.

Simon: Excellent. But if you work here, you'll need to post every Tuesday and Friday—by noon.

Ines: No problem. I'm very punctual.

Simon: Great. Now, we need someone right away. When can you start?

Ines: On Monday.

Simon: Perfect. Let me talk to my boss and I'll be in touch with you later this week.

> **ZOOMA MAGAZINE NEEDS STUDENT BLOGGERS!**
>
> You . . .
> - are 18–22.
> - know a lot about pop culture.
> - have good writing skills.
> - are punctual and can work independently.

 blog: an online diary

blogger: someone who writes a blog

B Practice the conversation in **A** with a partner.

5 Speaking Strategy

Useful Expressions: Interviewing for a job		
	The interviewer	**The applicant**
Starting the interview	Thanks for coming in today.	It's great to be here. / My pleasure.
Discussing abilities and experience	Tell me a little about yourself.	I'm a first-year university student. I'm majoring in journalism.
	Can you (work independently)? Are you (punctual)?	Yes, I can. For example, . . . Yes, I am. For example, . . .
	Have you ever (done this kind of work)?	Yes, I work for my school newspaper now.
Ending the interview	Do you have any questions?	Yes, I do. / No, I don't think so.
	When can you start?	Right away. / On Monday. / Next week.
	I'll be in touch.	I look forward to hearing from you.

A Imagine that you're applying for the student blogger job. Create a new dialog with a partner. Use the interview in Speaking and two or three Useful Expressions.

B Perform your conversation for another pair.

6 Language Link The present perfect; *for* and *since*

A Look at the time line. Then read sentences 1 and 2 below. Notice the verb forms in blue.

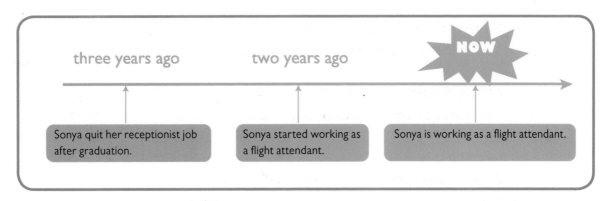

three years ago	two years ago	**NOW**
Sonya quit her receptionist job after graduation.	Sonya started working as a flight attendant.	Sonya is working as a flight attendant.

1. Sonya has worked as a flight attendant **for** two years.

2. She hasn't worked as a receptionist **since** graduation.

> Use the present perfect (*have / has* + past participle) for an action that started in the past and continues up to now.

B *For* and *since* are often used with the present perfect. Fill in the blanks with *for* or *since*.

1. ___For___ half an hour
2. ___since___ last year
3. ___since___ noon
4. ___For___ one month

5. ___since___ yesterday
6. ___For___ three hours
7. ___since___ I started the job
8. ___For___ decades

> **for** + a period of time:
> *for two years*
> **since** + a point in time:
> *since 2010*
> **since** + a past time clause:
> *since she graduated*

C Complete these profiles. Use the present perfect with the verbs in parentheses and *for* or *since*.

"I ___have lived___ (live) in the United States ___since___ August. I ___have studied___ (study) English ___since___ I was in high school. I'm studying for an exam right now. I ___haven't slept___ (not / sleep) well ___For___ two days. I ___have drunk___ (drink) three cups of coffee ___since___ 9:00."

"He ___has been___ (be) in college ___For___ three years. He ___hasn't come___ (not / come) home ___For___ a year. I miss him. He ___has lived___ (live) overseas ___since___ 2003. We ___haven't talked___ (not / talk) on the phone ___For___ a month."

D Use the verbs in parentheses to form questions. Then ask and answer them with a partner.

How long have you . . .

1. ___studied___ (study) English?
2. ___been___ (be) at this school?
3. ___know___ (know) your best friend?
4. ___had___ (have) the same hairstyle?

7 Communication I really want this job!

A Complete the job ads below with the qualities and abilities / experience needed. You can use the answers in the box more than once. Add your own ideas, too.

Qualities	Abilities / Experience	
	be able to . . .	**have experience . . .**
a fun, energetic person who loves the outdoors	swim well	caring for animals
good with computers	work flexible hours	working with children
patient and kind to animals	walk long distances	playing video games
a cautious, responsible person	work independently	
	speak English well	

Metro Classifieds Your Guide to Great Jobs

Work from home!
Part-time VIDEO-GAME TESTER needed!
Qualities needed: _____
_____
Abilities needed: _____
_____
Playing video games

WORK AS A SUMMER CAMP COUNSELOR
with kids ages 10-12 **IN THE U.S.!** 18
must be 18 years, must speak another language
Qualities needed: *A fun, energetic person who loves the outdoors.*
Abilities needed: *speak English well working with children.*

Weekend LIFEGUARDS needed now!
Qualities needed: *A _____ person*
Abilities needed: *swim well, work flexible hours.*

Afternoon DOG WALKERS needed Mon.—Fri.
Qualities needed: *Patient and kind to animals*
Abilities needed: *walk long distances caring for animals.*

B Choose a job in **A** to apply for. Tell your partner your choice. Then do the following:

- Complete the questions. Then use them to interview your partner. Take turns.

- After the interview, decide if your partner is good for the job. Why or why not?

> Thanks for coming in today. So, tell me ... what do you do now?

Interview questions
Name: *Leslie Hernandez*
Job he/she is applying for: *Afternoon Dog Walkers*

1. What do you do now? How long have you done it?
2. Are you *patient and kind* to animals? Give me an example.
   (quality)
3. Have you ever *take care dogs* ?
   (experience)
4. Can you *walk longs distances*? Please explain.
   (ability)
5. Your question: *Can you talking about your*

experience with dogs?

The World of Work

Lesson B   Dream jobs

1   Vocabulary Link   Not your typical job

A   Read about these people's jobs. Tell a partner: What does each person do?

I'm a crab fisherman in Alaska for part of the year. It's a physically demanding job—you work 12 to 14 hours a day, often in terrible weather. It's also one of the most hazardous jobs in the world—a lot of people die doing it every year. I do it because I can make a lot of money fast —about $50,000 for eight weeks of work. But it isn't steady work. After two or three months, I'm out of a job.

After graduation, I was in a dead-end job with no future. It was terrible. But now I've found a dream job. I work as a youth director on a cruise ship, organizing activities for kids. The job is really rewarding. When you teach kids to swim, for example, it feels really good. The job can be exhausting, though, because you're always busy. But the travel, plus working with a diverse staff from many different countries, means the job is never dull.

> ℹ️ **Word partnership** *job*
> (v.) apply for / be out of / get / look for / quit *a* **job**
> (adj.) a dead-end / desk / dream / full-time / part-time / steady **job**

B   Match a word or phrase in blue from **A** with its definition below.

1. dangerous _hazardous_
2. boring _dull_
3. satisfying, pleasing _rewarding_
4. unemployed _out of a job_
5. a perfect job _dream job_
6. continuing, not changing _steady_
7. varied, different _diverse_
8. hard, challenging _demanding_
9. a job with no hope for growth _a dead end job_
10. very tiring _exhausting_

C   Write the name of a job for each adjective in the chart. Compare your ideas with a partner.

type of job	name of job	type of job	name of job
physically demanding		dead-end	
hazardous		dull	
rewarding		dream	

> **ASK ANSWER**
> Look at the jobs in **A** and the ones you wrote in **C**. Which would you like to do? Which would you never do? Why?

2 Listening   **It's worth it.**

A   Gino is a storyboard artist. What do you think he does? Choose the best picture.

 ✓

CD 2
Track 20

B   Listen and check your answer in **A**. Then circle the true sentence about Gino's job below.

a. He illustrates comic books.   c. He draws pictures of events in a movie.

b. He draws pictures for children's books.   d. He takes photos of famous actors.

CD 2
Track 21

C   Read sentences 1–4. Then listen again and circle *True* or *False*.

Gino thinks . . .

1. the best part of his job is meeting famous people.	True	~~False~~
2. his job is dull sometimes.	True	~~False~~
3. working with a director is usually pretty easy.	True	~~False~~
4. it's common to work long hours in his job.	~~True~~	False

CD 2
Track 21

D   Gino gives people advice about becoming a storyboard artist. Which advice does he NOT give? Circle it. Listen again to check your answer.

a. Be knowledgeable about making films. ✓   c. Be a good artist. ✓

b. Be able to work independently.   d. Be a hard worker. ✓

ASK   ANSWER

Does Gino's job sound interesting to you? Why or why not?

3 Reading   **I love my job.**

A   Look at the photos. What do you think these people's jobs are?

B   Look quickly at the two interviews on the next page. Match a photo in **A** (1, 2, 3, or 4) with a person.

Jonas ____3____   Tye ____4____

C Read these job profiles. Then complete the summaries of Jonas's and Tye's jobs below. Use the words in the box. Three are extra.

Interview 1 - Name: Jonas

What do you do? I'm a V.J. or "video jockey."

How would you describe your job? I'm on TV. I introduce music videos and talk about them. I also interview singers who appear in videos.

What is the best part of your job? I get to meet a lot of famous people. That's very exciting. Also, I love music. This is definitely my dream job.

What is the worst part of your job? Well, it's fun meeting famous people, but some of them aren't very nice. They think they are better than me.

What was your most memorable moment? Last year, I presented an award on TV at a music awards show. I couldn't believe it. They flew me to Los Angeles and I stayed in Beverly Hills. I was on the TV show for a whole 45 seconds! I got to meet a lot of stars.

I want to be a V.J. How do I get the job? Well, first you have to make a video of yourself. You need to talk about certain things on the video. In my case, there was a list of questions, like "What did you do last weekend?" and "What's on your iPod right now?" After you talk about yourself, you send the video in to the TV station. They call you if they like it.

Interview 2 - Name: Tye

What do you do? I'm a car courier.

How would you describe your job? Sometimes a person or a company needs a car moved from one place to another. They may not have time to do it themselves. They hire me to drive the car.

What is the best part of your job? The freedom—I'm glad it's not a desk job. Also, I like to drive, so it's fun for me. Last summer, I drove all the way from New York to California. The weather was great. I had the music on and enjoyed my trip very much.

What is the worst part of your job? The schedule—it's demanding. If I say I'll arrive on Monday at 6:00, I have to be there by Monday at 6:00. Sometimes that means driving long distances in a short time. There are days when I work 12 to 14 hours straight. It can be exhausting and stressful.

What was your most memorable moment? I once drove a famous actor's car from Miami to New York City and he gave me a really big tip.[1] It was incredible!

I want to be a car courier. How do I get the job? That's a good question. My mother started this business, so she hired me. You'd have to call my mom to find out!

[1] **tip:** extra money you give someone for a service they've done

| tiring | mom | interviews | loves | unusual | hates |
| famous | punctual | introduces | moves | friend | video |

Jonas (1) _interviews_ singers and (2) _introduces_ music videos. He meets a lot of (3) _famous_ people. That's the good and the bad part of the job. He (4) _loves_ his job. He made a (5) _video_ to get his job.

Tye (6) _moves_ cars from one place to another. You have to be (7) _punctual_ to do his job and it can be (8) _tiring_. Tye's (9) _mom_ gave him the job.

D Work with a partner. One person will be Jonas and the other Tye. Read through your profile once more. Then follow the directions.

1. **Student A:** Ask your partner the six questions in the reading.

2. **Student B:** Cover the reading and answer your partner's questions in your own words.

3. Change roles and repeat steps 1 and 2.

4 Language Link Verb + infinitive

A Study the chart.

These verbs can be followed by another verb in the infinitive form (*to* + verb):					
agree	choose	forget	learn	need	start
arrange	decide	hate	like	plan	try
attempt	expect	hope	love	prepare	want

B Read each sentence. Then do the following:

- Underline the main verb.
- Which verbs are followed by an infinitive? Circle the infinitive forms.
  Not all the sentences have one.

1. They <u>plan</u> (to move) to Mexico.
2. I <u>chose</u> (to go) to a large university.
3. I <u>need</u> a snack before I <u>go</u> to bed.
4. I <u>like</u> (to buy) presents for my friends.

5. I <u>forgot</u> the key to this door.
6. He <u>hopes</u> (to meet) her parents.
7. I <u>expect</u> him at ten minutes to three.
8. Do you <u>want</u> (to work) in an office?

C Complete the sentences below with the infinitive form of the verbs in the box.
Check your answers with a partner.

go	help	open	~~speak~~	~~work~~	~~attend~~
~~become~~	~~graduate~~	~~perform~~	~~sing~~	~~work~~	

Sanjay: I've always liked (1) <u>to speak</u> foreign languages. I decided (2) <u>to work</u> as an interpreter. I work at the United Nations.

Teresa: I chose (3) <u>to go</u> to medical school because I wanted (4) <u>to help</u> people. I'm planning (5) <u>to work</u> in a clinic in my hometown.

Dan: My sister is learning (6) <u>to sing</u>. She wants (7) <u>to perform</u> in an opera someday.

Camille: I want (8) <u>to become</u> a flight attendant. I need (9) <u>to attend</u> a six-week training course. I expect (10) <u>to graduate</u> in August and start (11) <u>to work</u> in September.

5 Writing Writing about jobs

A Choose one of the topics below and write about it.

- a part-time or summer job you had
- your dream job

B Exchange your writing with a partner. Ask your partner one question about his or her job.

I like to swim so I decided to get a job last summer as a lifeguard. Many people applied for the job but I got it. For three months, I worked every day from 10:00 a.m. until 3:00 p.m.

6 Communication   Guess my job!

A   Get into groups of four: Students A, B, C, and D.
Get ready to play "Guess my job!" Read the instructions below.

taxi driver

flight attendant

rafting tour guide

ski instructor

film director

police officer

astronaut

forest ranger

fashion designer

1. Student A secretly chooses one of the jobs above. Don't say the job you choose!

2. Students B, C, and D take turns asking one question each to discover Student A's
   job. Use a verb from the box below or one of your own.

try	choose	want	learn	need	plan
attempt	expect	hate	like	hope	love

How do you learn to do your job?

3. Student A answers the three questions. Then together,
   Students B, C, and D take one guess to discover the job.

4. If the guess is incorrect, the game continues. Repeat steps 2 and 3
   until someone guesses correctly.

B   Take turns being Student A and play "Guess my job!" again.

Check out the World Link video.

Practice your English online at http://elt.heinle.com/worldlink

1 Storyboard

A Harry is telling Linda about his dream. Complete the story.
For some blanks, more than one answer is possible.

I had a very strange dream last night.

Really? What _____?

I _____ in the sky. It _____ very cold. In fact, it _____ .

Then suddenly, everything changed. I ____ on a farm.

We're having a party. Would you _____?

_____, but I can't. I'm in a hurry.

While the farmer was talking, I _____ a strange feeling . . . like I _____ into a hole.

Help!

Then I suddenly _____. I ____ on the floor and my window was open and it _____.

Wow! That's a really _____ dream.

Yeah, I know!

B Cover the story. Take turns telling it to your partner.

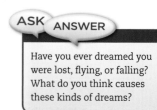

ASK ANSWER

Have you ever dreamed you were lost, flying, or falling? What do you think causes these kinds of dreams?

2 See It and Say It

A Yesterday there was a movie premiere at the Galaxy Theater. Look at the picture.
What were the people doing when the movie star arrived? Tell your partner.

PREMIERE

TONIGHT, 7:00!

GALAXY THEATER

PRESS

B Think of a movie you know. Write the name of the movie on the sign in the picture.
Invite your partner to the premiere. Your partner should ask one or two questions.

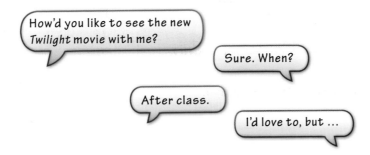

How'd you like to see the new *Twilight* movie with me?

Sure. When?

After class.

I'd love to, but ...

C Invite other friends to see the movie.
Practice inviting and accepting or refusing invitations.

3 Listening

CD 2
Track 22

A Read the information in the box. Then listen and complete each person's profile below. Use one word in each blank.

Every year, the Dream Big Foundation gives $10,000 to a person between the ages of 17 and 22 so that he or she can do something important—go to college, study abroad, start a business, etc. This year, the foundation received thousands of applications from all over the world. There are now two finalists—Teresa Silva and Daniel Okoye. Who should get the prize?

Name: Teresa Silva   **Age:** 21

What she does:
- She created a _____ to help poor artists sell their products to the _____.
- When a product sells, she takes _____ % and gives _____% to the artists.
- Since _____, she has already sold _____ items.

Why she needs the money:
- There's a lot of _____ to do.

What she plans to do with the money:
- She plans to _____ one more person.
- She hopes to sell _____ as many items.

Name: Daniel Okoye   **Age:** 18

What he does:
- He's a _____.

Why he needs the money:
- His parents _____ when he was _____.
- He has no money for _____.

What he plans to do with the money:
- He wants to study _____.
- He hopes to become a _____ and help others.

B You work for the Dream Big Foundation. Review your notes in **A**. Follow the directions.

- Which words in the box below would you use to describe Teresa and Daniel? Why?

- In your opinion, which person should win the money? Why? Give at least two reasons.

brave / courageous	cautious	clever	efficient	flexible
motivated / ambitious	careless	independent	pleasant	punctual

C Get into a group of 3 or 4 people. Compare your answers in **B**. Together choose the winner of this year's prize. Then share your answer with the class.

> I think Teresa should get the money because she's very clever . . .

> So do I.

> Yeah, but Daniel lost his parents as a teenager and . . .

4 Spot the Error

A Find and correct the mistake(s) in the sentences below. You have five minutes.

1. **A:** I really liked that movie.
   B: So am I.

2. After graduation, I hope visit my cousin in New York City.

3. Sorry I missed your call. I watched TV and I didn't hear the phone.

4. You seem quietly today. Are you OK?

5. Maya's worked for the same company since two years. Now she wants quit and get a new job.

6. **A:** How long you know John?
   B: Since high school. We are friends for many years.

B Compare your answers in **A** with a partner. If you have different answers, explain your corrections.

5 Speak for a Minute!

A Read the questions below and think about your answers.
Do not talk about your answers with anyone.

1. Talk about the last movie you saw. What was the story about?

2. Talk about a festival or holiday that you know. Where and when does it take place? What happens?

3. Which would you prefer to do—work for a company or work for yourself?

4. Talk about the last party you went to. What was it for? Who hosted it? Did you have a good time? Why or why not?

5. To speak English well, what do you need to do? What should you try not to do?

6. Name something you've wanted to do for a long time. Why haven't you done it yet?

B Work with 3 other people.

1. On six small pieces of paper, write a number 1 to 6.
   Put the six numbers in a hat or bag.

2. Take turns. Pick a question out of the hat or bag.

3. Answer the question. Talk for one minute without stopping and you get 1 point.

4. Continue until there are no more questions.
   The winner is the person with the most points.

Telecommunications
Lesson A Telephoning

1 Vocabulary Link   Give me a call.

A Tell your partner: What kind of cell phone do you have?
What do you like most about your phone?

B Look at the phrases in the chart. Then ask your partner:
Which phrases do you know? What do they mean?

Phrases with *phone*	Phrases with *call*	Phrases with *message*
answer the phone	call (someone)	check your (text / phone) messages
be on the phone	call (someone) back	get a (text / phone) message
hang up the phone	get a call (from someone)	leave a message
turn on your phone	make a call	send (someone) a text message
turn off your phone	screen (your) calls	take a message

C Complete the sentences below. Use the <u>correct form of a verb</u> in the chart. Use each verb only once.

1. Before the movie starts, please ____turn off____ your cell phones.

2. **A:** Carlos?
   B: Yeah, wait a minute . . . I'm _____ on the phone. I'm talking to Marta.

3. **A:** I heard the phone ring. Who called?
   B: It was probably a wrong number. When I __answer__ the phone and said, "Hello," the person __hung up__ .

4. **A:** Good morning, Barr and Associates.
   B: Mr. Choi, please.
   A: He's busy at the moment. Can I __take__ a message?
   B: No, thanks. I'll __call__ back later.

5. **A:** Ann, you __got__ a call from Bill earlier.
   B: Did he __leave__ a message?
   A: Yeah. He said to meet him at the library at 3:00.

6. **A:** Your phone is ringing. Aren't you going to answer it?
   B: No, I'm __screening__ my calls. I don't want to talk to Sam.

7. **A:** __check__ your messages. I think Mom called you.
   B: No, I haven't __received__ a message from her. Oh, wait—she __sent__ me a text message.
   It says, "Dinner at 7:00."

8. Can I use your phone for a minute? I need to __make__ a call.

D Discuss the questions with a partner.

1. Do you talk on the phone a lot?

2. In one day, how many calls do you make? How many texts do you get?
   How many texts do you send?

3. Do you always answer your phone or do you sometimes screen your calls?

2 Listening On the phone

A Read the sentences below. Then listen to six conversations. In each conversation, what would the man say next? Choose the best response.

CD 2
Track 23

1. a. OK, I'll check my messages.
   b. No, thanks. I'll call back later.
   c. Yes, I left a message.

2. a. Please leave me a message and I'll call you back.
   b. Would you like to leave a message?
   c. May I ask who's calling?

3. a. When is a good time to call?
   b. No, nobody called.
   c. Thanks, I will.

4. a. No, he sent me a text message.
   b. He can't come to class today.
   c. I don't know. He hung up.

5. a. Why? Are you screening your calls?
   b. No, can I take a message?
   c. Sorry, I think you have the wrong number.

6. a. Hang up and try the number again.
   b. Oh, I think my cell phone was turned off.
   c. No, sorry. I don't know the answer.

B Listen to the conversations again and check your answers.

CD 2
Track 23

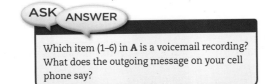

ASK ANSWER

Which item (1–6) in **A** is a voicemail recording? What does the outgoing message on your cell phone say?

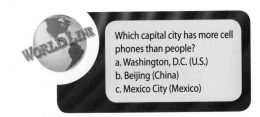

WORLD LINK

Which capital city has more cell phones than people?
a. Washington, D.C. (U.S.)
b. Beijing (China)
c. Mexico City (Mexico)

3 Pronunciation Repeating to clarify information

A Listen to this conversation. Notice the intonation of B's sentence. Why does B stress the underlined number?

CD 2
Track 24

A: My number is 555-6749.

B: 555-6749?

A: Yes. 6-7-4-9.

B Listen and complete the conversations. Then practice saying them aloud.

CD 2
Track 25

1. **A:** My number is 555-2526.
   B: Did you say 555-_____?
   A: No, it's 2-5-2-6.

2. **A:** My work number is 800-221-5348.
   B: _____?
   A: That's correct.

3. **A:** You can call me at 555-1661.
   B: Was that 555- _____?
   A: No, it's 1-6-6-1.

C Practice the conversations in **B** with a partner.
Then use your own phone number and practice again.

4 Speaking   **May I speak to Lisa, please?**

CD 2
Track 26

A   Celia and Lisa are chatting when their phone call is interrupted. Listen to the conversations. Which one is more formal?

Lisa:	Hello?
Celia:	Lisa? Hi. It's Celia.
Lisa:	Oh, hey, Celia. How're you doing?
Celia:	Pretty good. So, are you ready for the big test tomorrow?
Lisa:	Almost, but I have one question. . . . (phone beeps) Oh, Celia, . . . can you hang on? I've got another call coming in.
Celia:	Yeah, no problem.
Lisa:	Hello?
Prof. Larson:	Yes, hello. May I speak to Lisa Sanchez, please?

Lisa:	Speaking.
Prof. Larson:	Lisa, this is Professor Larson. You left me a message earlier today. You had a question about tomorrow's exam.
Lisa:	Oh, right. Professor Larson, could you hold for a moment?
Prof. Larson:	Of course.
Lisa:	Hello, Celia? Can I call you back? I have to take the other call.
Celia:	Sure. Talk to you later.

B   Practice the conversation in **A** with two classmates. Use your own names in the dialog.

5 Speaking Strategy

A   Make the conversation below more polite by changing the underlined words. Then practice it with a partner.

A: Hello?

B: Hi. Is Kurt there? _____

A: Who's calling?   *May I ask who calling?*

B: This is Martin.

A: OK, hang on. *Would you hold a moment?*
espere

B: Sure.
certo

A: Sorry, he's not in.
Can I take a message? _____

B: No, thanks. I'll call back later.

B   Create two phone conversations with your partner. One should be informal. The other should be more formal.

C   Perform your conversations for another pair. Can they guess which one is more formal?

Useful Expressions: Using the telephone	
Asking for someone & responding	Hi, Lisa? / Hi. Is Lisa there?
	Hello. May / Could / Can I speak to Lisa, please? [formal]
	This is Lisa. / Speaking.
Asking for identification of caller	Who's calling? *Quem está ligando*
	May I ask who's calling? [formal]
Asking someone to wait	Hang on. / Can you hang on (for a moment / second)?
	Would / Could you hold (for a moment / second)? [formal]
Taking a message	Can I take a message?
	May I take a message? [formal]
	Would you like to leave a message? [formal]

6 Language Link   Permission with *may, can, could, would / do you mind if . . .*

A   Study the chart. Then complete the sentences below with the correct word
or phrase from the chart. Sometimes more than one answer is possible.

Asking for permission		Responding
most formal ↑ **Would you mind if**	I used your phone?	No, not at all. / No, go ahead. Sorry, but . . .
Do you mind if		
May / Could least formal ↓ **Can**	I use your phone?	Certainly. / Of course. *Formal* Sure, no problem. / OK. *Informal* Sorry, but . . .

1. ___Do you mind if/May/Could/Can___ I use your dictionary? I need to look up a word.

2. _____ I borrowed your notes from yesterday's class? I was sick.

3. _____ I call you back in ten minutes? Someone is at the door.

4. Excuse me, Professor Walker._____ I talk to you for a minute?

5. It's cold in here._____ I closed the window?

6. _____ I sit here or is this seat taken?

7. _____ I made a phone call in here?

B   Work with a partner and do the following:

- Review your questions in **A**. Which ones were formal? Which questions were more informal?

- Take turns asking and answering the questions. Use the responses in the chart to help you.

C   Read each situation below. Use the verbs in parentheses to ask permission.

1. Your friend is doing his / her homework. You have finished your homework,
   and you want to watch TV. Ask permission very informally. (turn on)

   _____

2. You're invited to a party on Saturday night. You want your friend to go, too.
   Ask the host's permission a little formally. (bring)

   _____

3. You were sick yesterday and missed an important test in class. You want to
   take it this Friday. Ask your teacher's permission formally. (take)

   _____

4. Your teacher doesn't allow cell phones turned on in class. You just got an important text
   and need to read it. Ask your teacher's permission formally. (check)

   _____

D   With a partner, take turns asking and answering the questions in **C**.
Refuse (say *no* to) one request and give a reason why.

7 Communication Good news!

A Get into groups of three: Student A, Student B, and Student C. Read the instructions.

Student A: Choose one piece of good news from the list below.

☐ I bought a cool new scooter!   ☐ I got an "A" on my exam!   ☐ I've got two tickets to a concert!
☐ I found your lost wallet!   ☐ I got a new job!   ☐ your idea: _____

Student B: Have a piece of paper and a pen ready to write down a message.

Student C: Choose a reason you are busy from the list below.

☐ You're taking a nap.   ☐ You're out with friends.
☐ You're at the library.   ☐ your idea: _____

B Role play these three conversations.

Step 1: Student A wants to give some good news to Student C, but Student B answers the phone. Student B explains why Student C is busy and takes Student A's message.

A: Hello. May I speak to Bianca, please?

B: I'm sorry, she's taking a nap. Can I take a message?

A: Yes. This is Ernesto. Would you tell her I found her wallet?

B: Sure, no problem. What's your number?

A: It's . . .

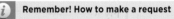

> **Remember! How to make a request**
>
> **Can/Could/Will/Would** you answer the phone?
>   OK. / Sure, no problem. / I'd be glad to.
>
> **Would you mind** answering the phone?
>   No, not at all. / No, I'd be glad to.

Step 2: Student B writes down the message and gives the information to Student C.

> :: WHILE YOU WERE OUT ::
> *Ernesto* **called.**
> **Time:** 12:30
> **Message:** *He found your wallet.*
> **Phone number:** 555-9733

Step 3: Student C calls Student A back to find out about the good news. Ask at least two questions.

C: Hi, Ernesto. It's Bianca.

A: Hi, Bianca. I have some good news. I found your wallet.

C: That's great! Where did you find it?

A: In the school cafeteria.

C: Thanks a lot, Ernesto. Could you bring it to school tomorrow?

C Switch roles so everyone gets a chance to play each role.

Telecommunications

Lesson B Cell-phone society

1 Vocabulary Link How polite are you?

A Read the quiz. Pay attention to the words and phrases in blue. Use your dictionary to help you.

High-Tech Etiquette: How polite are you?

1. You're on a date and you get a text from a friend. It says, "How's it going?" What do you do?

   ☐ Check it and respond right away.
   ☐ Ignore the message. Answering it now would be rude.
   ☐ My idea: _____

2. You're on the bus. The person next to you is listening to really loud music on his MP3. What do you do?

   ☐ Ask him to turn down the music. You don't want to hear it!
   ☐ Put on your headphones and turn up your music loud, too.
   ☐ My idea: _____

3. I think cell phones should be . . .

   ☐ banned in crowded places like subways and airplanes. No one should be able to use them.
   ☐ allowed everywhere. I should be able to make a call wherever I want to.
   ☑ My idea: _____

4. When talking on my cell phone in public (on the bus, in a restaurant), I usually . . .

   ☐ raise my voice so the caller can hear me clearly.
   ☑ lower my voice. I don't want others to hear my conversation.
   ☐ My idea: _____

5. You want to put some funny pictures of your friend on your social networking site, but the photos might make your friend uncomfortable. What do you do?

   ☑ Show your friend the photos first. It's the thoughtful thing to do.
   ☐ Just post the photos. If he doesn't like them, you can delete them.
   ☐ My idea: _____

the *Spiderman 2* sou
displaying considering
same-old sound that
intact — a sign of po
latter-day REM-song
Cure's new 21st cent

or refrain for the l
out of place in the

B Complete the chart of opposites with a word or phrase in blue from **A**. Then explain the meaning of the words with a partner.

> What does *respond* mean?

> Well, if you *respond* to a question, you answer it. The opposite is *ignore*.

Word	Opposite
respond	*ignore*
polite	
turn down	
banned	
raise your voice	
thoughtless	
add, post	

C Now take the quiz in **A**. Then explain your answers to a partner.

2 Listening   Do you mind?

CD 2
Track 27

A Read the items below. Then listen to the conversations and choose the best answers for each one.

Conversation 1

1. The speakers are in a _____.

   a. classroom
   b. restaurant
   c. movie theater

2. The man is asking the girl to _____.

   a. turn off her phone
   b. lower her voice
   c. turn down her music

Conversation 2

1. The speakers are _____.

   a. on a plane
   b. at a concert
   c. in a movie theater

2. After the woman talks to him, the man probably _____.

   a. listens to an announcement
   b. ends his phone call
   c. stops using his MP3

Conversation 3

1. The girl is worried because _____ on the website Linkbook.

   a. she doesn't have any friends
   b. a friend wrote an angry message to her
   c. she doesn't want to be friends with someone

2. What will the girl probably do next?

   a. become friends with Manny
   b. ignore Manny's request
   c. call Manny at home

B Listen to the conversations again. Then ask a partner:
What information in each conversation helped you choose your answers?

CD 2
Track 27

ASK ANSWER

Think about the situations in the three conversations. Have these things ever happened to you?

3 Reading   Phone free in the car?

A Read the title and first paragraph on page 111. Then tell a partner:
What new law passed recently? Is the law working?

B Read the readers' comments. Then match each person with his or her opinion. (Two readers have the same opinion.)

C Look at your answers in **B**. Why does each person have this opinion? Give a reason for each person from the reading.

Person	Opinion
Simon	Some cell-phone use in the car should be allowed.
Alexis	
Yalun	All cell-phone use in the car should be banned.

1. Simon: _____

   _____

2. Alexis: _____

   _____

3. Yalun: _____

   _____

NewsOnline

World   National   Regional   Business   Technology   Science

Phone free in the car?

Back to article »

A new law passed recently. It bans all cell-phone use while you are driving—including talking on the phone, texting, and e-mailing. The fine[1] for breaking the law[2] is high, but many drivers are ignoring the ban. What do you think about this problem?

Add your comment

Readers' Comments

Look—I've got a cell phone, and I'm glad to have it. But come on! Talking on the phone or texting while you're driving is crazy. And yet, I see people doing **things like this** every day. Using your cell phone and driving at the same time causes accidents . . . or worse. There have been many studies to prove this. My question is: Where are the police? **They** don't seem to care, so it's easy for drivers to ignore the law. When people are afraid of getting a large fine, cell-phone use in the car will stop. Everyone needs to learn that when you drive, you should turn off your phone. It's very simple! ~Simon

OK, I agree—texting or having a long phone conversation while driving is hazardous. But can we really ban all cell-phone use in cars? For example, yesterday I was driving home and I saw an accident on the road. I made a call and reported **it**. Did I stop driving to make the call? No. But did I help someone? Yes. We need to talk more about this new law. I just don't think the answer to the problem is so simple. ~Alexis

I don't think we can ban all cell-phone use in cars—especially if you use a hands-free device while driving, like I do. Look, I listen to the radio in my car. Isn't the music distracting[3]? Sometimes my friend is in the car with me. I talk to her while I'm driving. Isn't **that** dangerous? I mean, isn't talking on the phone (hands-free) the same as listening to music or talking to a passenger? In my opinion, they ARE all the same, and so I think we should be able to chat on the phone while we're driving. ~Yalun

---

[1] A **fine** is money you pay when you break a law.   [3] If something is **distracting**, it makes it hard to pay attention.
[2] If you **break a law**, you do something illegal.

D   Look at the highlighted words in the passage and complete the sentences with the correct answer.

ASK ANSWER

Whose opinion(s) do you agree with? Why?

In the reading, . . .

1. *Things like this* means _____.
   a. talking on the phone while driving   b. texting while driving   c. both a and b

2. *They* means _____.
   a. the drivers   b. the police   c. both a and b

3. *It* means the _____.
   a. accident   b. driver   c. call

4. *That* means _____.
   a. talking while driving   b. using a hands-free device   c. listening to music

4 Language Link   Verb + gerund vs. verb + infinitive

A   Read the note on the right and study the chart.

Verbs followed by infinitive only		Verbs followed by gerund only		Verbs followed by gerund or infinitive	
agree	plan	appreciate	feel like	can't stand	prefer
choose	prepare	avoid	finish	continue	start
decide	seem	can't help	imagine	like	try
hope	want	dislike	keep	love	*get*
learn	would like	enjoy	suggest	*talk*	
need	*get*	(not) mind	*talking*	*work*	

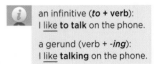

an infinitive (*to* + verb):
I <u>like</u> **to talk** on the phone.

a gerund (verb + *-ing*):
I <u>like</u> **talking** on the phone.

B   Notice the use of the gerund or the infinitive in each sentence. Check (✔) the sentences that are correct. Change the incorrect sentences.

1. ☑ I learned to speak Spanish when I was four.

2. ☑ I avoid to use cell phones in public places.

3. ☑ I like playing sports.

4. ☑ I appreciated to receive such a beautiful gift.

5. ☑ I agreed turning down the music on my MP3.

6. ☑ I prefer to respond to messages quickly.

do mind = not ok

can't stand = hate

C   How do you feel about the activities below? Use the verbs in the box with the phrases in parentheses to write sentences.

avoid   hate   need   can't stand   enjoy   like   (not) mind   want

1. (study on weekends) __I hate to study on weekends.__

2. (talk on the phone) __I need to talk...__

3. (get wrong numbers) __I can't stand get wrong numbers__

4. (eat junk food) __I avoit eat junk food__ *to*

5. (cook at home) __I enjoy cook at home__

6. (go to the beach) __I like to go to the beach__

D   Compare your ideas in **C** with a partner.

> I hate to study on weekends.

> Me, too. I can't stand studying on weekends.

5 Writing   Opinions about cell phones

A   Look back at question 3 on page 109. Then, on a separate piece of paper, complete the information in the box.

I think cell-phone use should be _____

Reason: _____

Reason: _____

Concluding sentence: For these reasons, I think . . .

> I think cell phones should be banned in places like subways and airplanes for two important reasons. First, these places are very small and crowded. People often raise their voices when they talk on the phone. Imagine everyone talking on their phones at once. How noisy! Second . . .

B   Use your outline in **A** to write a short paragraph like the example on the right.

C   Exchange papers with a partner. Are your opinions similar or different?

6 Communication How young is too young?

Do you think young children should have cell phones? Why or why not?

A Take this quiz about children and cell phones. Compare your answers with a partner. Then check your answers on page 154. Are any of these statistics similar in your country?

Cell Phone Quiz

1. A survey in the U.S says ___ of 8- to 12-year-olds have a cell phone.

a. 4%

b. 21%

c. 45%

2. A study in Britain says that cell phones may be dangerous for children's ___.

a. brains

b. ears

c. voices

3. A recent law in Bangladesh says that children under 16 cannot ___ cell phones.

a. buy

b. sell

c. use

4. In Japan, more than 80% of teenagers and ___ of junior high school students have cell phones.

a. 5%

b. 25%

c. 60%

B Evan is twelve years old. He wants a cell phone. Read what each person thinks about the situation.

Evan Logan

"I want to get a cell phone. All my friends have one. I need one to make phone calls and play games."

Mrs. Logan

"I can't relax unless Evan has a phone. I want to be able to reach Evan immediately if I have to."

Mr. Logan

"Why does a 12-year-old need a cell phone? He's a kid! He should be playing, not making phone calls."

Evan's doctor

"Cell phones are convenient, but it may not be safe for children to use them a lot."

C Get into groups of four. Each student role plays a person in **B**. Discuss whether Evan should get a cell phone. What is your group's final decision? Explain it to the class.

Dad, I want to get a cell phone. All my friends have one!

Evan, you don't need to have a cell phone. I think you should wait until you're sixteen to get one.

 Check out the World Link video.

 Practice your English online at http://elt.heinle.com/worldlink

11 Technology Today

Lesson A   Then and now

1 Vocabulary Link   **They make life easier.**

A Read the ads. Pay attention to the words in blue. Then match the sentence parts below to form correct definitions. One answer is extra.

Trend → tendencia

Do you want to take digital photos without spending a lot of money on a new camera?

Try DR Digital.
It lets you take 50 photos for only $25!

Why should you buy the DR Digital?

- It's reliable: You can trust DR Digital to work like a regular camera—for a lot less money!
- It's durable: Dropped it on the floor or got water on it? No problem. This camera keeps working!
- It's portable: It's small and lightweight, and it goes with you everywhere!
- It's disposable: Use it once—at a party, a wedding, or on vacation. When you're done, put it in the recycling bin!

*recycling bin = container in which glass, paper, and plastic are collected for reuse.

Are you tired of wearing glasses or contact lenses?

Now, there's a third choice —
LASIK eye surgery.

Why should you choose LASIK?

- It's convenient: It's done in a doctor's office and takes only 30–60 minutes. The result: better vision!
- It's practical: LASIK makes sense. Think of all the money you'll save on glasses or contacts!
- It's affordable: LASIK doesn't have to be expensive. Talk to us about a low-cost payment plan!

 The suffix *-able / -ible* = can.

If something is *affordable*, you can afford it.

What do you think the words below mean? What are their opposites?

breakable   separable
predictable   visible

1. If something is affordable, . . .   it costs a lot of money.
2. If something is convenient, . . .   you can probably buy it.
3. If something is practical, . . .   it makes life easy or more comfortable.
4. If something is disposable, . . .   you can carry it from one place to another easily.
5. If something is durable, . . .   you can trust it.
6. If something is portable, . . .   you throw it away after you've used it.
7. If something is reliable, . . .   it is a useful and logical thing to do.
                                               it is strong and lasts a long time without breaking.

B Discuss the questions with a partner.

1. Choose <u>one</u> of the ads in **A** and answer the questions. Use your own words.
   a. What is the ad selling?   b. Why should you buy it?

2. Would you ever have LASIK eye surgery or use a disposable camera? Explain your answer. Do you think these things make our lives better? Why or why not?

3. Which words in blue in **A** would you use to describe your MP3 player? Phone? Car?

2 Listening · Predicting the future

A How do these two items make our lives more convenient? Tell a partner.

B Read the questions and answers below. Then listen to the lecture and choose the best answer for each.

CD 2
Track 28

1. In the 1940s, the president of IBM made a prediction about computers. What was it?
   a. They will never be popular with most people.
   b. Someday, they will be small and portable.
   c. In the future, people will use them in their homes.

2. In the 1980s, seeing movies changed. What happened?
   a. Movie tickets became more affordable.
   b. People began watching movies online.
   c. Renting movies became popular.

3. In the 1980s, people were making a prediction about movies. What was it?
   a. All movie theaters will close.
   b. Someday, all movies will be free.
   c. No one will watch movies anymore.

4. What prediction are people making today?
   a. In the future, people won't make movies.
   b. In the future, people won't watch traditional TV.
   c. Someday, everyone will use computers.

5. Look at your answer in 4. Why are people making this prediction?
   a. More people are getting news and entertainment online.
   b. Movies are becoming too expensive.
   c. Computers are becoming cheaper.

ASK ANSWER

Look at your answers to questions 1 and 3. Were these predictions correct? Why or why not?

Look at your answers to questions 4 and 5. Do you agree with this prediction? Why or why not?

3 Pronunciation · Pronunciation of *s* in *used to* and *use / used*

CD 2
Track 29

A Listen to the sentences. Notice the different pronunciation of the *s* in *used to* and the *s* in the verb forms *use* or *used*.

used to / didn't use to: s = /s/	use / used: s = /z/
1. People used to go to movie theaters a lot more.	3. What kind of computer do you use?
2. I didn't use to wear glasses.	4. I used my brother's cell phone.

B Listen to how the words *use* and *used* are pronounced. Check (✔) */s/* or */z/*. Then take turns reading the sentences aloud with a partner.

CD 2
Track 30

	/s/	/z/
1. She <u>used</u> the phone in her office.	☐	☐
2. He <u>used</u> to paint his own house.	☐	☐
3. Do you <u>use</u> a laptop?	☐	☐
4. I didn't <u>use</u> to eat meat.	☐	☐

4 Speaking — The fact is . . .

CD 2
Track 31

A Listen to Alan and Kim's conversation.
Then answer the questions with a partner.

1. How would most people describe Kim's sister?

2. What is Kim's sister really like?

Alan: Hey, Kim. I saw your sister on Facebook the other day. She's really changed a lot.

Kim: Yeah? Why do you say that? She still looks the same.

Alan: Yeah, but now she's got all these friends and she's really funny. She used to be so different—you know, kind of shy.

Kim: A lot of people say that about my sister. They think that she's this quiet person, but, actually, she's very outgoing.

Alan: Really?

Kim: Yep. Once she feels comfortable with you, she's really friendly and she talks a lot.

Alan: Wow, I had no idea.

B Practice the conversation with a partner. Do you know anyone like Kim's sister?

5 Speaking Strategy

Useful Expressions: Stating facts		
Stating what other people think	A lot of people say (that) . . . Some people think (that) . . .	she's really shy.
Explaining what you think	(But,) actually, . . . (But,) in fact, / in reality, . . . (But,) the truth / fact / reality is . . .	she's very outgoing.

A Read the statements below and check (✔) the ones you agree with.

____ Learning English is easy.

____ Playing video games is bad for you.

____ You should get married some day.

____ The more expensive something is the better quality it is.

____ Computers make our lives better and easier.

____ Men are more aggressive than women.

B With a partner, compare your opinions about the statements in **A**. Talk about the statements you <u>don't</u> agree with. Use the Useful Expressions to help you.

> Some people say learning English is easy, but, actually, it's hard—especially the grammar.

C Tell a partner something surprising about you or your country.

> A lot of people think it's warm in Spain all year, but, in reality, it's very cold in the winter.

> Wow, I had no idea.

6 Language Link   *Used to*

A   Study the chart. Notice the different forms of *used to*. Then complete sentences 1-3 below.

> We use *used to* to talk about situations that were true or happened regularly in the past. These situations are not true now or do not happen anymore.
>
> **A:** This computer used to be really expensive.
> **B:** I know, but now most people can afford it.
>
> **A:** Did your brother use to spend a lot of time on Linkbook?
> **B:** Yeah, he used to, but he doesn't anymore.

1. Use *used to* to talk about the _____.   a. present   b. past

2. *Used to* is followed by _____.   a. the base form of a verb   b. a gerund (*-ing* form)

3. Use *use to* in negative statements and _____.   a. responses   b. questions

B   Each sentence below contains one mistake. Correct the mistakes. Then compare answers with a partner.

1. I use to talk on the phone a lot.

2. Did you used to have long hair?

3. My computer never use to crash so often.

4. Didn't you used to wear glasses?

5. We used live in the city, but we moved last year.

6. He never used to watching TV.

C   With a partner, use the verbs in the box to describe each situation in Mary's life ten years ago and now. Use *used to* and the simple present.

listen to	go to	wear
watch	work on	

1 Before: hip-hop music / Now: jazz

2. Before: glasses / Now: contacts

3. Before: movie theater / Now: DVDs at home

4. Before: large PC / Now: small laptop

> Mary used to listen to hip-hop music. Now she ...

D   Look again at the pictures and ask your partner: How else has Mary's life changed?

7 Communication   Things have changed.

A Two years ago, Tetsuya and his family moved from Tokyo to Los Angeles. Look at his old Tokyo web page and his new Los Angeles web page. How has his life changed? Make sentences with *used to* and *didn't use to*.

> People used to call him Tetsuya. Now everyone calls him . . .

Tokyo Homepage

- My name is Tetsuya.
- I live in Tokyo with my parents.
- I wear a uniform to school.
- I ride my bicycle to school.
- I belong to the soccer club.
- I study all the time, but my English isn't very good.

last updated: three years ago

LA Homepage

- Everyone here calls me "Ted." I like L.A. a lot.
- Guess what? I have a new niece! Her name is Risa.
- I don't wear a uniform.
- I have a car! I drive to college.
- I'm a member of my college's swim team.
- I have a lot of friends and we speak English together!

last updated: yesterday

B Make notes about your life five years ago and now. Try to write down things that are different if possible.

Five years ago	Now
Home: _____	Home: _____
Family: _____	Family: _____
Friends: _____	Friends: _____
Work / School: _____	Work / School: _____
Favorites (movies, magazines, TV programs): _____	Favorites (movies, magazines, TV programs): _____
Other: _____	Other: _____

C Tell your partner how your life has changed in the past five years. Whose life — yours or your partner's — has changed the most?

> My family and I used to live in a small apartment. Now we live in a bigger place.

Technology Today

Lesson B   Making life better

1   Vocabulary Link   **Too much plastic**

A   Read the information. Then match a word or phrase in blue with its definition below.

What is the Great Pacific Garbage Patch?

It's an area of water located in the Pacific Ocean. It is hundreds of kilometers wide and is filled with trash—most of which is plastic.

Why is this area a problem?

- It is killing animal and plant life.

- Eventually, it may have a negative effect on humans. For example, fish that consume plastic because they think it is food, won't be safe for people to eat.

What are scientists doing about the problem?

They're trying to …

- prevent the growth of this area. We can stop it, they say, if we use less plastic and recycle plastic goods we already have.

- rescue injured or sick animals in the area.

- use advanced technology to transform the plastic so that it breaks down faster. In time, this will reduce the amount of plastic in the area to almost nothing. Eventually, scientists hope to restore the area to its original, cleaner state.

plastic bottles and other trash

Garbage at sea
The Great Pacific Garbage Patch is created by plastic debris and other trash from around the world that is brought together by ocean currents.

Source: NOAA
Graphic: Andrea Maschietto, San Jose Mercury News   © 2009 MCT

1. a specific place   _____area_____
2. stop something from happening   _____
3. decrease   _____
4. save   _____
5. reuse   _____
6. change something completely   _____
7. eat or drink   _____
8. have a bad influence   _____
9. found in a certain place   _____
10. make something like it was in the past   _____

> **Notice!**
>
> **effect** = a noun | **affect** = a verb
>
> Scientists are studying the effect of TV on children.
>
> This problem affects everyone.

ASK   ANSWER

In addition to recycling, how else can we reduce the amount of plastic we use?

B   Read the information in **A** again. Then with a partner, take turns asking the three questions in the reading. Use your own words to answer.

2 Listening   Now you see it.

A Complete the sentences below with the words *blind*, *sight*, and *vision*. Use your dictionary to help you.

1. _____ or _____ is the ability to see things.

2. If you are _____, you can't see.

a computer chip

B Look at the photos and read the sentences below.
Then listen and choose the best answer to complete each one.

CD 2
Track 32

1. The man is talking about a tool he and others are working on. This tool will _____.
   a. prevent blindness from happening
   b. restore blind people's vision
   c. give blind people perfect vision

2. The glasses have a _____ inside.
   a. computer chip   b. pen   c. video camera

a pair of glasses

C How does the tool work? Read the sentences below.
Then listen again and put the steps in the order (1-5) they happen.

CD 2
Track 32

_____ The person can see the pen.

_____ The blind person puts on special glasses and looks at an object, such as a pen.

_____ The picture is sent to the chip in the person's eye.

_____ Doctors put a computer chip in a blind person's eye.

_____ The glasses take a picture of the pen.

> **ASK ANSWER**
>
> Use your answers in **B** and **C** to explain how this new technology works. What do you think of this tool?

3 Reading   Rescue robots

A Read the title of the news article on page 121. Look also at the photos and read the captions. What do you think this article is about? Tell a partner. Then read the article to check your ideas.

B Find the four bold words in the passage and read the sentences they are in. Then match each word with its definition. One definition is extra.

Word	Definition
collapsed	discovered
trapped	put something down
position	fell down
identified	unable to escape or move
	location, place

C Morgan is telling people what happened to her. Number the events (1-9) in the order they happened.

_____ They took me to the hospital.

_____ Then the roof of the gym fell down, and I passed out.

_____ I went into the gym for my class.

_____ I have to stay for a couple of days, but I'm feeling much better!

_____ Then suddenly, this little robot appeared.

_1_ It was snowing really hard on Tuesday morning.

_____ A few minutes later, a couple of men found me.

_____ When I woke up, I tried to move, but I couldn't. I was scared.

_____ I heard this really loud sound.

The Fairview Herald

Local Girl Rescued

She may have a broken leg, but she couldn't be happier. Morgan Bailey, 15, is happy to be alive.

Tuesday was like any other day for Morgan. She was at school. It was fourth period, and she was the first student to arrive in the gymnasium for her physical education class.

Suddenly there was a loud noise.

"There was a sharp cracking noise and then a loud boom. After that, I don't remember anything," said Morgan. "I guess I passed out[1]."

The roof of the gymnasium had **collapsed** under the heavy snow. Morgan was **trapped** underneath. She couldn't escape.

"I woke up and there was a big piece of wood on my leg. I couldn't move it. I was starting to get cold."

Fortunately, help was nearby. A new program using "rescue robots" was tried for the first time.

"We were nervous about using the robot," said Derrick Sneed, the man in charge of the program. "But in the end, the robot gave us reliable information. It went extremely well."

The rescue robot was able to go into the gym and locate Morgan's exact **position**.

"We send in robots first because it may not be safe for humans," said Mr. Sneed. "People are not as useful as robots in some situations. A gas leak, for example, could kill you or me but wouldn't hurt a robot."

Although it didn't happen in Morgan's case, some rescue robots can bring fresh air or water to people who are trapped.

Rescue robots go into rough, dangerous places. They work in life-or-death situations. They have to be durable.

"Once we **identified** Morgan's location and knew it was safe, a couple of our men went in to rescue her," says Sneed. "Her leg was broken and she was scared, but thankfully, she was alive."

Doctors say that Morgan is doing well. She should be going home in two or three days. What is the first thing she wants to do after she gets out of the hospital?

"I want to meet my hero," laughs Morgan, "That little robot saved my life!"

[1] If you **pass out**, you become unconscious.

Rescue robot

A dangerous mess

D Imagine you are Morgan and you're talking to reporters. With a partner, use your answers in **C** and take turns retelling her story. Use your own words.

ASK ANSWER

In what other kinds of situations could rescue robots be used?

4 Language Link   *As . . . as*

A The photos below show a regular vacuum cleaner and two robotic ones.
Read the sentences in the box. Then answer questions 1-3 with a partner.

> • The Roomba weighs as much as the Vacuum Cleaner Pro.
>
> • The regular vacuum cleaner is not as light as the Roomba or the Vacuum Cleaner Pro.
>
> • The regular vacuum cleaner doesn't cost as much as the Roomba or the Vacuum Cleaner Pro.

a regular vacuum cleaner

the Roomba

the Vacuum Cleaner Pro

9 kilos / $80   **4 kilos / $130**   **4 kilos / $130**

1. Which vacuum cleaners weigh the same? What phrase in the box is used to show this?

2. Which vacuum cleaner is the cheapest? What phrase is used to show this?

3. Which vacuum cleaners cost the same? How can you say this using *as . . . as*?

B Look at the comparisons below. Use the words in parentheses to write sentences using *as . . . as*.
Then check your answers with a partner.

	regular vacuum cleaner	the Roomba
1. expensive	☐	☐
2. work well	☐	☐
3. durable	☐	☐
4. easy to use	☐	☐
5. popular	☐	☐

1. (vacuum cleaner) *A regular vacuum cleaner isn't as expensive as the Roomba.*

2. (the Roomba) _____

3. (the Roomba) _____

4. (vacuum cleaner) _____

5. (the Roomba) _____

5 Writing   **Comparing two products**

A Read the paragraphs. What two things is the writer comparing? Which one does she like more? Why?

B Think of two similar products. Choose from the list below or use your own idea. Then write a short paragraph. Explain which product you think is better.

> two MP3s   two cell phones
>
> two video games   two similar websites

> I used to own an iListen, but two months ago, I got an iTouch. Of the two MP3s, I like the iTouch better.
>
> With the iTouch, I can listen to music, watch and make videos, play games, surf the Web, and many other things. The iListen doesn't have as many features. Also, the iListen's battery doesn't last as long as the iTouch's. And finally, . . .

C Exchange papers with a partner. Answer the questions in **A** about your partner's writing.

6 Communication **Design your own robot.**

A With a partner, design a robot that will do something useful for people. Discuss the questions below.

1. What is the purpose of the robot? Choose from the list below or write your own idea.

to be a friend to children or adults	to do household chores
to work in schools	to work in hospitals
to do factory work / to build things	other: _____

Paro is a Japanese robotic toy used in hospitals. It looks like a seal and helps to reduce stress in patients.

2. What will the robot do?

3. What will the robot look like? Draw a simple picture on a separate piece of paper.

4. Why is the robot as good as (or better than) a human?

5. What will you call the robot?

B Get together with another pair and take turns doing the following.

Presenters: Present your robot.

Listeners: As you listen to the other pair's presentation, complete "Pair 1" in the chart below. At the end of the presentation, you may ask questions.

	Pair 1	Pair 2	Pair 3
Robot's name			
What it does			
Why the robot is as good as (or better than) a human			
Would you use this pair's robot? Why or why not?			

C Repeat **B** with two other pairs. When you have finished, compare notes with your partner and choose your favorite robot. Explain your choice to the class.

 Check out the World Link video.

 Practice your English online at http://elt.heinle.com/worldlink

1 Vocabulary Link   Tasks before a trip

A Andrew and Becky are going on a trip. What will they do before they leave home? Match 1-5 with a-e. Then match 6-10 with f-j.

1. unplug	a. the trash	6. give	f. the house keys to a friend
2. empty	b. money	7. stop	g. the plants
3. exchange	c. the bills	8. turn off	h. the lights
4. give away	d. any electrical items	9. confirm	i. the mail delivery
5. pay	e. any fresh foods	10. water	j. the flight plans

B Look at the pictures. With a partner, take turns telling what Andrew and Becky did. Use the vocabulary in **A**.

I'm calling to confirm our flights to …

Please hold our mail for three weeks.

Thank you. Here are the keys. Do you want this fruit?

Andrew called to confirm the flight plans.

Becky called to . . .

C Discuss the questions with a partner.

1. Think of a trip you've taken. Which tasks did you do before you left home?

2. What might happen if you forget to do some of the tasks in **A**?

2 Listening   While we're away, could you . . . ?

A Paula is asking Leticia for help. What does she ask Leticia to do? Check (✔) the task.

CD 2
Track 33

☐ feed the dog   ☐ pick up the mail   ☐ water the plants

> **i** kennel = a place where pets stay when their owners leave town

B Listen again. Write *P* for Paula or *L* for Leticia.

CD 2
Track 33

1. __P__ is taking a trip for two weeks.
2. ____ is going to water the plants.
3. ____ is going to put the dog in the kennel.
4. ____ asked about the mail.
5. ____ stopped the mail delivery.
6. ____ will give the keys to ____.

> **ASK** **ANSWER**
> Do you ever ask your friends or neighbors for help? Why or why not?

> **WORLDLINK**
> Which is the busiest air route in the world?
> a. Paris to New York City
> b. Hong Kong to Taipei
> c. Rio de Janeiro to Lisbon

3 Pronunciation   Reduced *have to* and *has to*

A Listen to these sentences. Notice the reduced pronunciation of *have to* and *has to*.

CD 2
Track 34

1. I'm going to miss my flight. I have to hurry.
2. Everyone has to sit down before this plane can take off.

B Imagine that you and a friend are going on a trip to another country.
How will you prepare? Make a list of tasks you and your friend have to do.

I have to . . .	My friend has to . . .

C Now tell a partner about the tasks. Use the reduced form of *have to* and *has to*.

> I have to pack my suitcase.

> My friend has to get some traveler's checks.

4 Speaking · I can't remember where it is.

CD 2
Track 35

A Mina and Esther are preparing to leave on a trip. Listen to their conversation. What is the problem?

Esther: We have to leave in thirty minutes. Have you finished packing?

Mina: Yes, I have . . .

Esther: You look worried. What's wrong?

Mina: I can't remember where I put my passport.

Esther: Oh, no!

Mina: It's here somewhere.

Esther: When did you last have it? →

Mina: About ten minutes ago. Let me think . . . Oh, there it is. I put it on the dresser.

Esther: What a relief! → *interjection*
                                        (alivio)

B Practice the conversation with a partner.

ASK **ANSWER**

Talk about a time when you lost something. What did you do?

5 Speaking Strategy

A Study the Useful Expressions in the chart. Practice saying the sentences.

Useful Expressions	
Saying you've forgotten something	
I forgot + noun	I forgot my bus pass.
I forgot + infinitive	I forgot to empty the trash. *to leave*
I don't remember + gerund	I don't remember turning off the lights.
I can't remember where + clause	I can't remember where I put my car keys.

B You are going to perform a short conversation about forgetting something. Follow the steps below.

Step 1: Choose a location.

☐ the airport
☐ school
☐ the office

Step 2: Choose something you forgot to take or do.

☐ ticket   ☐ get traveler's checks
☐ report   ☐ feed the dog
☐ textbook   ☐ other: _____

Step 3: Write and practice a short conversation with your partner. Then perform it for the class.

> OK, it's time to get on the plane.

> Oh, no! I forgot my ticket.

6 Language Link   Modal verbs of necessity

A Study the chart. Then complete sentences 1-4 below with a partner.
For one sentence, more than one answer is possble.

Use *must*, *have to*, and *have got to* to say that something is necessary.		
	Present forms	**Past forms**
affirmative	You must show your ID to get on the plane. I have to buy a backpack for my trip. We have got to get some cash.	I had to wait at the airport for an hour.
negative	I don't have to check any luggage.	I didn't have to wait long.

1. You can use _____ in the present to express necessity.

 a. must   b. have to   c. have got to

2. Only _____ can be used to talk about things that were necessary in the past.

 a. must   b. have to   c. have got to

3. _____ is often used to talk about rules or laws. It is stronger than *have (got) to*.

 a. Must   b. Have to   c. Have got to

4. You can only use _____ in the negative.

 a. must   b. have to   c. have got to

B These people are preparing for a trip. Look at their lists. They have finished the
tasks that are checked (✔). On a separate piece of paper, write eight sentences
with *has / have to* or *doesn't / don't have to*. Compare your answers with a partner.

Jake

Jim and Doris

✓ buy a backpack
  prepare a first-aid kit
  get shots
✓ apply for a youth hostel card

✓ exchange money
✓ pay the bills
  change the voicemail message
  stop the mail delivery

C Correct the error in each sentence.

1. She doesn't has to pack her suitcase.

2. They must leave yesterday.

3. I haven't to reserve a hotel.

4. All passengers must to board the flight now.

5. We didn't had to pay in cash.

6. You don't have got to buy traveler's checks.

A   Imagine you and your partner are going on a camping trip for three days. You will be in the forest, far away from any towns or cities. With your partner:

- Circle the items that are necessary for your trip.
- Check (✔) the items that you would like to bring, but that are not necessary.
- Cross out the items that are not necessary.

chewing gum

sleeping bag

cell phone

flashlight

bottled water

canned food

backpack

Swiss army knife

FIRST AID KIT

first-aid kit

lighter

money

thermos bottle

cooking pot

plastic plates
and cups

tent

B   Join another pair. Together you must decide what to take on your trip. You can only take six items. Choose four items pictured above. Think of two more items. Consider these things:

- food
- shelter
- safety
- water
- first aid

> We have to take the tent for shelter.

C   Tell the class the items your group has decided to take and explain your reasons.

Let's Go Somewhere!

Lesson B Adventures in traveling

1 Vocabulary Link   Airline travel

 A Match a word on the left with one on the right to form compound nouns about air travel. Write each compound noun below the picture it describes. Then check your answers with a partner.

baggage	carry-on	flight	oxygen
boarding	check-in	overhead	tray

attendant	compartment	luggage	pass
claim	counter	mask	table

   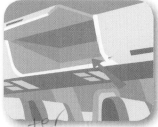

1. _____tray table_____   2. boarding Pass   3. check in Counter   4. comparm

   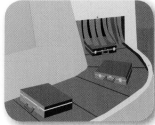

5. flight attendant   6. oxigen mask 7. carryon luggage 8. baggage claim

B Use the compound words in **A** to complete the sentences below.

1. When you arrive at the airport for your flight, you go to the ___check-in___ ___counter___ first.

2. When your departing flight is announced, pick up your carry on luggage and go to the gate.

3. Before you get on the plane, you must show your boarding pass

4. When you enter the plane, you put your luggage in the overhead com pament You may need to ask a ___flig___ for help.

5. Before takeoff, you learn about safety. They show you how to use an oxigen mask in an emergency.

6. During the flight, you are served drinks on your ___ta_____.

7. After the flight is over, you go to the _____ _____ area to get your luggage.

ASK ANSWER
Have you ever been on a plane?

2 Listening   A long weekend

> Many students and workers look forward to a holiday that happens on a Monday or Friday because they can enjoy a "long weekend." What do you like to do on a long weekend?

A Listen. What did Jun do? Circle the correct answers.

CD 2
Track 36

Jun flew / drove to three / four countries in three / four days.

B Listen again. Check (✔) the statements that are true for Jun.

CD 2
Track 36

☐ 1. Jun loves flying.

☐ 2. Jun didn't go shopping.

☐ 3. Jun was in a hurry.

☐ 4. Jun had two pieces of luggage.

☐ 5. Jun didn't make a reservation.

☐ 6. Jun's flights were expensive.

☐ 7. Jun works for an airline.

☐ 8. Jun works in sales.

ASK ANSWER

Would you like to take a trip like Jun's? Why or why not? Where would you like to go on a long weekend?

WORLD LINK

The shortest scheduled flight in the world is between the Isle of Westray and Isle of Papa Westray in Scotland. How long is this flight?
a. 2 minutes
b. 15 minutes
c. 20 minutes

3 Reading   Traveling alone

> Would you like to take a vacation by yourself? Why or why not?

A Read the title of the article on page 131. What do you think the author is writing about? Check (✔) your answer. Then read the article and see if you were right.

☐ 1. the advantages of traveling alone

☐ 2. some memories of traveling alone

☐ 3. the expense of traveling alone

B Read the article again. What topics does the author mention about solo travel? Check (✔) your answers.

☐ 1. the cost of solo travel

☐ 2. the dangers of traveling alone

☐ 3. study vacations

☐ 4. using your vacation to learn a sport

☐ 5. packing for a trip alone

☐ 6. options for solo travelers

130   **LESSON B** • Adventures in traveling

GOING SOLO IS THE WAY TO GO!

by D. Toor

How do you usually travel? Do you go with a close friend or a group of friends? Do you join a tour group? Do you travel with your family?

Have you ever imagined "going solo"? In the mid 1990s, it was estimated that 9 million Americans were planning a summer vacation alone. Since then, the number of solo travelers has increased.

You may think that traveling alone would be scary or boring. Well, according to people who do it, that's not exactly true. Solo travelers often have positive experiences: they make new friends, get to know themselves better, and can make their own schedules.

There are many different things you can do on a vacation alone. Some solo travelers use the time to learn or practice a sport such as golf, mountain climbing, or scuba diving. Others go and stay on a ranch and learn how to ride a horse. You can pretend to be a cowboy or a cowgirl for a day!

You may not believe this, but some travelers like to study on their vacation. They even go to "vacation college" at a university or join a research team as a volunteer worker. It's hard but satisfying work. You can "play scientist" for a week or two while you help someone with their project.

For solo travelers of different ages and genders, there are many travel options. There are tours for women only and for people over the age of 60. And, of course, there are trips for singles who are looking for romance. One company offers trips that focus on fine dining—there is time for sightseeing during the day and for sharing a delicious meal with new friends at night.

The next time you take a trip somewhere, why don't you consider going solo?

Bon voyage!

C Look at the items you checked in **B**. For each item, give examples from the reading.

1. _____

2. _____

3. _____

ASK ANSWER

What would you do on a vacation by yourself?

What cities do you think are good destinations if you're traveling solo? Why do you think so?

4 Language Link   The present perfect for indefinite time

A   Study the chart. Notice how the present perfect is used in the conversations.

The present perfect is used to talk about past actions, when the time they happened is unknown or unimportant.		
Questions	**Answers**	
Have you **ever** been to Brazil?	Yes, I have. I <u>was</u> there two years ago. No, I haven't. Have you?	*ever* = at any time in the past up to now **Notice!** When you mention a specific time (yesterday, two years ago), use the <u>simple past</u>.
Have you packed **yet**?	Yes, I've already packed. No, I haven't packed yet. / No, not yet.	Use *already* in affirmative statements. Use *yet* in questions and negative statements.

B   Read each conversation and the statement below.
Write *T* for true, *F* for false, or *N* for not enough information.

1. **Man:**　Do you want a sandwich?
   Woman: I've already eaten, thanks.

   • The woman is hungry. ___F___

2. **Woman:** Have you ever visited Rio?
   Man:　Yes, I have.

   • The man went to Rio last year. ___N___

3. **Man:**　Should I call a cab for you?
   Woman: No, Fred has already called one.

   • A cab was called. ___T___

4. **Woman:** What does Maria want?
   Man:　I don't know, but she's called three times.

   • Maria called an hour ago. ___N___

5. **Man:**　Have you been to London?
   Woman: I haven't. But I've been to the UK twice.

   • The woman visits London often. ___F___

6. **Woman:** Have you put the suitcases in the car?
   Man:　Not yet.

   • The suitcases are in the car. ___F___

5 Writing   Travel experiences

A   Write about a place you've visited.

   • Describe the things you did.

   • Explain why you liked or didn't like the place.

B   Exchange papers with a partner.

   • Have you ever visited the place in your partner's writing?

   • Ask your partner one question about the place he or she visited.

I've been to Barcelona, a city in Spain. It's a great city. I was there last summer for a month. I was studying Spanish at a school and I lived with a host family.
   In Barcelona, I visited many famous sites, such as La Rambla and . . .

6 Communication **Find someone who has . . .**

 A Follow these instructions.

1. Ask your classmates questions with the present perfect.
   Complete as much of the chart as you can.

2. When someone answers "Yes" to a question, ask another question to get more information.
   Then write the person's name and the piece of information in the chart.

> Jin Sung, have you ever visited a big city?

> Yes, I have.

> Which city?

> Seoul.

Find someone who has . . .

	Find someone who has . . .	Name	Information
❶	visited a big city	Sofia	Yes. I have. To N.Y
❷	joined a group tour	Haya	No, I don't
❸	talked to a flight attendant	Sofia	Yes. I do.
❹	ridden on a train	Rony	Yes. I have. Paris to Amster-
❺	gone on a trip and forgotten something	Lubina	Yes. I have. She forgot her silver
❻	spent time on a beach	Carlos	Yes. His favorite is playing Blanca
❼	participated in a festival	Rony	Yes, I have. Kite festival
❽	seen a TV show about a foreign place	Sofia	Yes. Her favorite is the early from up
❾	eaten food from another country	Sofia	Yes. Vietnamise food
❿	overpacked for a trip	Maria	Yes, I have. all time
⓫	gone on a day trip	Carlos	Yes. A lot. To Mochima park
⓬	taken a lot of photos of something	Maria	Yes. I have. I like take photos

 B Get to know your classmates. Listen to your teacher read each item in **A**. If you've ever done the activity, raise your hand.

 Check out the World Link video. Practice your English online at http://elt.heinle.com/worldlink

Review: Units 10–12

1 Storyboard

A Pia is calling Bob, her boss, at work. Complete the conversation. For some blanks, more than one answer is possible.

 B In groups of three, practice the conversation. Then change roles and practice again.

 C Think of an interesting place to make a telephone call from. Then make your own conversation like the one above. Practice with your group.

2 See It and Say It

A Look at the picture of Leo's house. He went on a trip, but he forgot to do many things before he left. On a separate piece of paper, make a list of what he forgot to do.

 B Pretend you are Leo and call a friend. Choose three things you forgot and ask for help. Then switch roles.

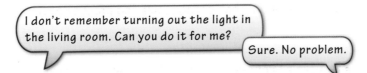

> I don't remember turning out the light in the living room. Can you do it for me?

> Sure. No problem.

3 A TV Ad

A Read the ad. Circle the correct verb forms in the sentences. Then unscramble the adjectives. Check your answers with a partner.

50 in / 127 cm

★ Are you planning (buying / (to buy)) a new TV?
★ Can't stand ((viewing) / to view) movies on a small screen?
★ When you watch sports, do you want (feeling / (to feel)) like you're actually at the game?
★ Would you like ((saving) / to save) energy when you watch TV?

Try our new flat screen HDTV!

And you'll appreciate (watching / to watch) TV in a whole new way!

★ _____ (cellxente) *picture quality!*
★ _____ (roffadable) *Now only $900!*
★ _____ (venconient) *Easy to use and perfect for any room in your home!*

B With a partner, compare your TV to the one in the ad using *(not) as . . . as.*

> My TV is not as expensive as the TV in the ad.

4 Old Favorites

A Complete the chart with your favorites.

	When you were younger	Now
Snack food		
Music group or singer		
Piece of clothing you own(ed)		
Hobby		
Weekend activities		

B With a partner, ask and answer questions about your present and past favorites. Use *used to* for the past favorites. Have you changed a lot?

> What snack food did you use to eat?

> I used to eat a lot of sweets, but these days, I eat healthier snacks.

5 First Trip

A Emma Goldstein is ninety years old. She took her first trip on an airplane last month. Read what she said. Then correct the mistake(s) in each sentence. It can be a mistake in grammar or vocabulary.

1. I used to ~~was~~ *be* afraid of flying.

2. Last month, I made a call from my daughter.

3. She said, "You must to pack your bags. We're taking a trip."

4. I didn't want to going at first because I disliked to fly.

5. I took two pieces of boarding passes on the plane.

6. The flight attendant was nice. She helped me put everything in the oxygen mask.

7. Airplane travel is not as scarier as I thought.

8. I can now proudly say, "I have flying on an airplane!"

B Ask your partner about a trip he or she has taken.

6 Listening

CD 2
Track 37

Read the phone messages below. Then listen and circle the correct answer for each question.

1. What message did Sheila leave for Tom?

WHILE YOU WERE OUT	**WHILE YOU WERE OUT**	**WHILE YOU WERE OUT**
Sheila called. She wants to meet soon. She will call again at 5:00.	Sheila called. She can't meet tomorrow. Please call her.	Sheila called. She can't meet today. She wants to meet tomorrow at 2:00.

2. What message did Ted leave for Penny's brother?

WHILE YOU WERE OUT	**WHILE YOU WERE OUT**	**WHILE YOU WERE OUT**
Ted called. His computer crashed and won't start. He wants you to fix it. Can you call him? His number is 555-9083.	Ted called. He has a question about his new laptop. Please call him back.	Ted called. He wants you to help him buy a new computer. He'll call you later.

Language Summaries

Unit 1 All About Me

Lesson A

Vocabulary Link

acquaintance
attend/go to (a school)
close friends
co-worker
date (someone)/go out (*with*
someone)
just friends
work together

Speaking Strategy

**Introducing a person to
someone else**

I'd like to introduce you to
  Andres.
I'd like you to meet Andres.

Junko, this is Ricardo.
Junko, meet Ricardo.
Junko, Ricardo.

Responding to introductions

It's (very) nice to meet you.
  (It's) nice/good to meet you,
  too.

Nice/Good to meet you.
  You, too.

Lesson B

Vocabulary Link

get a good - bad grade
have (*name of sport*) practice
meet (*for* a time/*on* a day)
pass - fail (an exam/a class)
prepare (*for* something)
take a class
take a lesson
tutor

Unit 2 Let's Eat!

Lesson A

Vocabulary Link

delicious/tasty
fried
juicy
salty
spicy
sweet
tastes like

Speaking Strategy

Making suggestions

Let's have Thai food.
Why don't we have Thai food?
How/What about having Thai
  food?

Responding to suggestions
Great idea!
(That) sounds good (to me).
Fine with me.
I don't really want to.
I don't really feel like it.

Lesson B

Vocabulary Link

a (balanced/healthy) diet
a (bad/unhealthy) habit
benefit
cut back (*on* something)
eat out
eliminate
increase
lifestyle
plenty (*of* something)
protect (*against* something)

Unit 3 Unsolved Mysteries

Lesson A

Vocabulary Link

by accident - on purpose
good luck - bad luck
lucky/fortunately - unlucky
luckily - unfortunately
miss a chance - take a chance
reunite - separate
work out (for the best)

Speaking Strategy

Talking about possibility

Saying something is likely

I bet (that) Marco plays drums.
Marco probably plays drums.
Maybe/Perhaps Marco plays drums.

Saying something isn't likely

I doubt (that) Marco plays drums.

Lesson B

Vocabulary Link

explain/explanation
figure out
investigate/investigation
make sense
mystery/mysterious
prove/proof
solve/solution
theory

Unit 4 Today's Trends

Lesson A

Vocabulary Link

a quarter/one-fourth/ twenty-five percent
almost/nearly
average
drop/decrease
half/fifty percent
over
percent
rise/increase
thousands
trend
twice/two times as high as (something else)

Speaking Strategy

Disagreeing

Politely
I know what you're saying, but …
Sorry, but I disagree. / I don't agree.
I hear you, but …

Strongly
That's not true.
I totally/completely disagree.
Oh, come on! / Are you serious?

Lesson B

Vocabulary Link

a look/style
in (style)/**out** (of style)

(body) piercings
baggy/oversized
casual
conservative
dramatic (hairstyle, makeup)
retro
ripped (clothes, jeans)
pointy (shoes, boots)
skinny/fitted (jeans)
sloppy
sporty

Unit 5 Out and About

Lesson A

Vocabulary Link

do the chores
do the dishes
do the laundry
go grocery shopping
mail (something)
make a reservation
make an appointment
make dinner
pick up – drop off (something)
run an errand
sweep (the floor)
take (someone) to (a place)
take a break
take the dog for a walk
vacuum (a rug)

Speaking Strategy

Making appointments

Explaining why you're calling

I'm calling to make a dental
appointment.
I'd like to make a dental
appointment.

Scheduling the time

Can you come in tomorrow
at 2:00?
Can you make it tomorrow
at 2:00?
How/What about tomorrow
at 4:00?

> That's perfect. / That works
> great.
> No, that day/time isn't good
> for me.

Lesson B

Vocabulary Link

ways to travel
by bike, bus, car, plane, subway,
    taxi, train
on foot
catch/take a bus, cab, plane,
    subway, train
ride a bike

talking about time
It takes . . . (+ time period)
a short time - a long time
(be) on time - (be) running late
pass (the) time (doing something)
spend time (*with* someone)

commute
stuck in traffic

Unit 6 Student Life

Lesson A

Vocabulary Link

admit/admission
apply to (a school)/
    application
apply for (something)/
    application
compete/competition
decide/decision
get into/get accepted to
    (a school)
graduate/graduation
recommend/
    recommendation

Speaking Strategy

Offering another point of view

I didn't get into Yale.

> Look on the bright side …
> Well, the good news is …
> Look at it this way …
> Yes, but on the other hand …
> (Yes, but) then again …

> three other schools accepted
> you.

Lesson B

Vocabulary Link

Definite time expressions
after graduation/school/work
in two hours/days/months
next week/month/year
this summer/spring/fall/winter
the day after tomorrow

Indefinite time expressions
in a few days
in the near future
someday/one of these days
soon
sooner or later

Unit 7 Let's Celebrate

Lesson A

Vocabulary Link

a host
celebrate/celebration
get presents
get together (*with* others)
have/throw/host a party
have a good time
invite (someone to something)
plan a party
root for (something or someone)
wild/rowdy

Speaking Strategy

Inviting someone to do something

Do you want to go with me?
Would you like to go with me?
How'd you like to go with me?

Accepting or refusing an invitation

Sure, I'd love to.
That sounds great.

I'm sorry, but I can't. I have plans.
Unfortunately, I can't. I have class.
I'd love to, but I'm busy.

Lesson B

Vocabulary Link

be held/take place
full (*of* something)
gather
participate/participation/
  participant
perform/performance/
  performer
race
win/winner
(win) a contest
(win) first prize

Unit 8 Storytelling

Lesson A

Vocabulary Link

a (TV/drama) series
a soap opera

a true story
be based on (a true story)
make up (a story)
tell a story
the same old story

a happy ending
be hooked on (something)
character
follow (something or
  someone)
predictable
realistic

Speaking Strategy

Telling a story

Introducing the story
It's (a story) about …
The story begins/starts in …
One day, …

Continuing the story
So (then), …
Later, …
After that, …
It turns out that …

Ending the story
In the end, …
Finally, …

Lesson B

Vocabulary Link

brave
clever
eventually
incredible/unbelievable
overcome
struggle
survive
uneducated

Unit 9 The World of Work

Lesson A

Vocabulary Link

cautious
courageous
efficient
flexible
independent
knowledgeable
pleasant
punctual
unpredictable

Speaking Strategy

Interviewing for a job

Thanks for coming in today.
    It's great to be here. / My
    pleasure.

Tell me a little about yourself.
    I'm majoring in journalism . . .

Have you ever (done this kind of
work)?
    Yes, when I was in college.

When can you start?
    Right away. / On Monday.

I'll be in touch.
    I look forward to hearing
    from you.

Lesson B

Vocabulary Link

a dead-end job
a dream job
be out of a job
demanding
diverse
dull
exhausting
hazardous
rewarding
steady

Unit 10 Telecommunications

Lesson A

Vocabulary Link

phone
answer the phone - hang up
be on the phone
turn on - turn off your phone

call
call (someone) back
get a call (*from* someone)
make a call
screen your calls

message
check your messages
get a message
leave a message
send a text (message)
take a message

Speaking Strategy

Using the telephone

Hi. Is Lisa there?
Hello. May/Could/Can I speak to
Lisa?
    This is Lisa. / Speaking.

Who's calling?
May I ask who's calling?

Hang on.
Can you hang on (for a moment)?
Would/Could you hold (for a
    moment)?

Can I take a message?
May I take a message?
Would you like to leave a
    message?

Lesson B

Vocabulary Link

allowed - banned
delete - add
ignore - respond
lower your voice - raise your
    voice
polite - rude
thoughtful - selfish/thoughtless
turn up - turn down

Unit 11 Technology Today

Lesson A

Vocabulary Link

affordable
convenient
disposable
durable
portable
practical
reliable

Speaking Strategy

Stating what other people think

A lot of people say (that) …
Some people think (that) …

Explaining what you think

(But,) actually, …
(But,) in fact,/in reality, …
(But), the truth/fact/reality is …

Lesson B

Vocabulary Link

affect/effect
area
consume
locate/location
prevent
recycle
reduce
rescue
restore
transform

Unit 12 Let's Go Somewhere!

Lesson A

Vocabulary Link

confirm the flight plans
empty the trash
exchange money
give away fresh foods
give the house keys to a friend
pay the bills
stop the mail delivery
turn off the lights
unplug electrical items
water the plants

Speaking Strategy

Saying you've forgotten something
I forgot + noun:
   I forgot my bus pass.
I forgot + infinitive:
   I forgot to empty the trash.

I don't remember + gerund:
   I don't remember turning off
    the lights.

I can't remember where + clause:
   I can't remember where I put
    my car keys.

Lesson B

Vocabulary Link

baggage claim
boarding pass
carry-on luggage
check-in counter
flight attendant
overhead compartment
oxygen mask
tray table

Grammar Notes

Unit 1   All About Me

Lesson A   Language Link: The simple present vs. the present continuous

I always **take** a shower in the morning. The express train **arrives** at 9:03 a.m. They **don't** **speak** Italian. They **speak** French.	Use the simple present to talk about habits, schedules, and facts.
Clara **isn't** **studying** right now. She**'s** **talking** on the phone at the moment.	Use the present continuous to talk about actions that are happening at the time of speaking. Notice the time expressions.
How many classes **are** you **taking** this term? Hiro **is living** in Singapore these days.	Also use the present continuous to talk about actions happening in the extended present (nowadays). Notice the time expressions.

Lesson B   Language Link: Review of the simple past

Subject	Verb		Time expressions	
I You	**missed** **didn't miss**	a tennis lesson	yesterday. two days/weeks ago. last week/month.	The past tense ending of regular verbs is -ed. For irregular verbs, see the list on the next page.
He/She We They	**had** **didn't have**			

	Yes / No questions	Answers
With *be*	Were you in class today?	Yes, I was./No, I wasn't.
With other verbs	Did you pass the test?	Yes, I did./No, I didn't.

	Wh- Questions	Answers
With *be*	Where were you last night?	(I was) at my friend's house.
With other verbs	When did you meet your girlfriend?	(We met) last year.

Regular past tense verbs				Irregular past tense verbs			
Base form	**Past tense**	**Base form**	**Past tense**	**Base form**	**Past tense**	**Base form**	**Past tense**
change	changed	pass	passed	be	was/were	know	knew
die	died	play	played	come	came	make	made
enter	entered	prepare	prepared	do	did	meet	met
finish	finished	practice	practiced	eat	ate	read	read
graduate	graduated	study	studied	give	gave	run	ran
help	helped	talk	talked	get	got	take	took
live	lived	travel	traveled	go	went	think	thought
marry	married	use	used	have	had	win	won
move	moved	work	worked	keep	kept	write	wrote

Unit 2   Let's Eat!

Lesson A   **Language Link:** The comparative form of adjectives

This restaurant is **bigger than** that one.	Use the comparative form of an adjective to compare two things.
Your cooking is **better than** my mom's. My cold is **worse** today **than** it was yesterday.	The comparative of *good* is *better*. The comparative of *bad* is *worse*.
I'm tall, but Milo is **taller**.	Sometimes, you can use the comparative form without *than*.

One syllable	sweet/sweet**er**	Add *-er* to many one-syllable adjectives.
	large/large**r**	Add *-r* if the adjective ends in *-e*.
	big/big**ger**	Double the final consonant and add *-er* if the adjective ends in a vowel + consonant.
Two syllables	simple/simple**r** quiet/quiet**er**	Add *-r* or *-er* to two-syllable adjectives that end in an unstressed syllable.
	spicy/spic**ier**	Change the final *-y* to *-ier* if the adjective ends in *-y*.
	crowded/**more** crowded famous/**more** famous	Add *more* to other adjectives, especially those ending in *-ing*, *-ed*, *-ious*, or *-ful*.
Three syllables	relaxing/**more** relaxing delicious/**more** delicious	Add *more* to all adjectives with three or more syllables.

Lesson B Language Link: The superlative form of adjectives

It's **the oldest** restaurant in Paris. (= The other restaurants are not as old.)	Use the superlative form of an adjective to compare something to an entire group.
It's **one of the oldest** restaurants in Paris. (= It's one of many old restaurants in Paris.)	Use *one of …* to show that something or someone is part of a group.
Mario's has **the best** pizza in the city. It was **the worst** movie of the year.	The superlative of *good* is *the best*. The superlative of *bad* is *the worst*.

One syllable	sweet/**the sweetest** large/**the largest**	Add *the* and *-est* or *-st* to many one-syllable adjectives.
Two syllables	quiet/**the quietest** simple/**the simplest**	Add *the* and *-est* or *-st* to two-syllable adjectives that end in an unstressed syllable.
	spicy/**the spiciest**	Add *the* and change the final *-y* to *-iest* if the adjective ends in *-y*.
	crowded/**the most** crowded famous/**the most** famous	Add *the most* to other adjectives, especially those ending in *-ing ,-ed*, *-ious*, or *-ful*.
Three syllables	relaxing/**the most** relaxing delicious/**the most** delicious	Add *the most* to all adjectives with three or more syllables.

Unit 3 Unsolved Mysteries

Lesson A Language Link: Stative verbs

He **seems** like a nice person. Not: ~~He is seeming like a nice person.~~	Stative verbs describe states and feelings (not actions). Usually, they are not used in the present continuous.
I <u>think</u> he is dangerous. [think = believe] I <u>am thinking</u> about the problem. [think = consider]	Some stative verbs (for example, *have, feel, look, see, think*) can be used in the continuous. When used this way, their meaning changes.
She <u>has</u> a lot of money. [have = own, possess] She's <u>having</u> coffee with a friend. [have = drink]	

Lesson B Language Link: Modals of present possibility

Subject	Modal	Main verb		
Luis	**may** **might** **could**	be	sick. He's not in class today.	Use *may*, *might*, and *could* to say something is possible.
	can't **couldn't**	be	sick. I just saw him in the cafeteria.	Use *can't* or *couldn't* to say something is not possible.

	Questions	Short answers
With *be*	Is Ian from the UK?	He might/could be. He can't/couldn't be.
With other verbs	Does Marta have a brother?	She might/could. She can't/couldn't.

Unit 4 Today's Trends

Lesson A **Language Link:** Quantity expressions

	With count nouns			With noncount nouns		**Quantity expressions** are used to talk about amounts.
100%	**All of**	my friends live with their parents.		**All of**	my homework is finished.	*a couple* = two Don't use *a couple* (*of*) with noncount nouns.
	Most of			**Most of**		
	A lot of			**A lot of**		
	A couple of			_____		
0%	**None of**			**None of**		

General	**Most students** work hard. [students everywhere]	*Most*, *some*, and *all* can be used to make general statements about people or things everywhere. Notice the difference between the sentences in each pair.
Specific	**Most (of the) students** <u>in my class</u> work hard.	
General	**Some families** have children. [families everywhere]	
Specific	**Some (of the) families** <u>in my neighborhood</u> have children.	
General	**All teachers** are strict. [teachers everywhere]	
Specific	**All (of the) teachers** <u>at my school</u> are strict.	

Lesson B **Language Link:** Giving advice with *could*, *should*, *ought to*, and *had better*

You **should/ought to** wear a suit to your job interview. You **shouldn't** wear jeans. They're too casual.	Use *should* or *ought to* to give advice. Use *shouldn't* in the negative.
You **could** wear a suit to the interview. You **could** wear your blue suit or the black one.	Use *could* to make a suggestion. It isn't as strong as *should* or *ought to*. *Could* is often used when there is more than one choice.
You**'d better** leave now or you'll miss your flight. We**'d better not** drive to the concert. It will be hard to park.	Use *had better* (*not*) to give strong advice. It sounds like a warning.

Unit 5 Out and About

Lesson A Language Link: Polite requests with modal verbs and *mind*

Making requests				Responding to requests
informal	**Can/Will** you **Could/Would** you	help	me, please?	OK./Sure, no problem. / I'd be glad to./Certainly. / Of course. Sorry, but …
formal	**Would you mind**	helping		No, not at all./No, I'd be glad to. Sorry, but …

- Use *Can you*, *Will you*, *Could you*, or *Would you* + verb to make requests.
- To make a formal request, use *Would you mind* + verb+ *-ing*.
  Note: To agree to a *Would you mind* … request, answer with *No.* (*No, I don't mind.*)
- To make a request more polite, add *please*.

Lesson B Language Link: Intensifiers: *really*, *very*, *pretty*

	Adverb	Adjective		*Really*, *very*, and *pretty* make adjectives and adverbs stronger.
I (don't) live	really/very	close	to school.	
I live	pretty			*Really* and *very* are stronger than *pretty*.
	Adverb	Adjective	Noun	
I (don't) have	really/very			Only *really* or *very* can be used in the negative.
I have	a	pretty	long	commute.
	Adverb	Verb		*Really* can come before a verb. *Very* cannot.
I (don't)	really	like	my new bike.	

I don't know John **at all**. (I've never met him.) I didn't like that movie **at all**.	You can use *at all* with negatives to mean *zero* or *never*.

Unit 6 Student Life

Lesson A Language Link: Plans and decisions with *be going to* and *will*

Subject + *be*	(not)	*going to*	Verb		Time expressions	Use *be going to* to talk about definite future plans (plans you have already made).
I'm You're He's/She's We're They're	not	going to	attend	Harvard	next month/year. this fall. in the summer. after graduation.	

	Contractions
A: What are your plans for today? **B:** I don't know. Maybe I**'ll** <u>see</u> a movie. **A:** Are you feeling OK? **B:** No, not really. Maybe I **won't** <u>go</u> to class today.	Use *will* to talk about a sudden decision (one you make as you're speaking). *Will* is followed by the <u>base form of a verb</u>. *Won't = will not*	I'll = I will you'll = you will he'll = he will she'll = she will we'll = we will they'll = they will

Lesson B Language Link: Predictions with *be going to* and *will*

Leo gets all As. I'm sure he**'s going to**/he**'ll** get a scholarship to college. She didn't study. I bet she **isn't going to**/she **won't** pass the test.	You can use *be going to* and *will* to make predictions about the future. It's common to use *I'm sure* and *I bet* when you make a prediction you are certain about.
He'll probably get a scholarship to college. She probably won't pass the test. Maybe we'll find a cure for cancer someday.	You can use *probably* or *maybe* when you aren't 100% sure about your prediction. *Probably* is stronger than *maybe*.
Look! That rock **is going to** fall.	Use *be going to* (not *will*) to make a prediction about an action that is about to happen very soon.

Unit 7 Let's Celebrate

Lesson A Language Link: Similarity and agreement with *so*, *too*, *either*, *neither*

	Affirmative answers	Negative answers
With *be*	I <u>am</u> going to Sayuri's party. **So am I./I am, too./Me, too.**	I'm <u>not</u> going to Sayuri's party. **Neither am I./I'm not, either./Me, neither.**
Other verbs	I <u>need</u> a costume for the party. **So do I./I do, too./Me, too.**	I <u>don't have</u> a costume for the party. **Neither do I./I don't, either./Me, neither.**

- Use the expressions above to show similarity or to agree with something said.
- *Me, too* and *Me, neither* are common in casual conversation.

Lesson B Language Link: Time clauses with *before*, *after*, and *when*

Time clause	Main clause	
Before the party,	you put on a costume.	A time clause explains when something happens. It is always connected to a main clause. A time clause can come before or after the main clause.
Main clause	**Time clause**	
You put on a costume	before the party.	

After she had dinner, Paloma went to bed.	Use *after* in a time clause to show that the event happened first. (Paloma had dinner, and then she went to bed.)
Before I left, I turned off the lights.	Use *before* in a time clause to show that the event happened second. (I turned off the lights, and then I left.)
When you see a friend, you say, "Hello."	Use *when* to show that the two events happen at the same time or one happens immediately after the other.

Unit 8 Storytelling

Lesson A Language Link: Past continuous vs. simple past

Subject	be	Verb + *-ing*		
I He/She	**was**(n't)			Use the **past continuous** to talk about an action in progress in the past.
You We They	**were**(n't)	**watching** TV	at 8 o'clock last night.	

A: I <u>called</u> you last night. **B:** I <u>didn't hear</u> the phone. I **was watching** TV.	Use <u>the simple past</u> (not the **past continuous**) to talk about a completed action. Use only the simple past (not the past continuous) with stative verbs (*be, hear, need, know, etc.*).
I **was taking** a shower *when* the phone <u>rang</u>. *While* I **was taking** a shower, the phone <u>rang</u>.	You can use the past continuous with the simple past to show that one action was in progress when another happened. Notice the words *when* and *while*.

Lesson B Language Link: Adverbs of manner

Cinderella danced **happily** with the prince. He speaks twelve languages **fluently**.	**Adverbs of manner** tell how something is done. They often come after a verb and end in *-ly*.
He was <u>different</u> from other children. Mary seems <u>unhappy</u>.	Remember: <u>Adjectives</u>, not adverbs, come after stative verbs (*be, have, hear, need, know, seem*, etc.).
She drives too **fast**. He often works **late**. They didn't do **well** in school.	Some common adverbs of manner don't end in *-ly*. Some examples are *fast, hard, late*, and *well*.

Unit 9 The World of Work

Lesson A Language Link: The present perfect; *for* and *since*

Subject	*have/has*	Past participle		*for/since* phrase
I/You/We/They	**have**(n't)	**lived**	here	for five years. since graduation.
He/She	**has**(n't)			

- Use the **present perfect** for an action that started in the past and continues up to now.
- For many verbs, the past participle is the same as the simple past form. Some irregular past participles are in parentheses: *be (been), go (gone), did (done), begin (begun)*.

Contractions

I've = I have
you've = you have
he's = he has
she's = she has
we've = we have
they've = they have

Questions	Answers
How long **have** you **lived** here? How long **has** she **lived** here?	(I've lived here) **for** two years. (She's lived here) **since** June 20. **since** she graduated.

for + a period of time
since + a point in time
since + a past time clause

Lesson B Language Link: Verb + infinitive

I **like** <u>to sing</u>. I **wanted** <u>to become</u> a singer. I **was planning** <u>to move</u> to New York. Then I got a job in London so I **needed** <u>to move</u> there.	Certain verbs can be followed by an <u>infinitive</u> (*to* + verb). Some examples are *agree, arrange, choose, decide, expect, forget, hate, hope, learn, like, love, need, plan, prepare, start, try*, and *want*. Note: The **main verb** can be in different tenses.

Unit 10   Telecommunications

Lesson A   **Language Link:** Permission with *may*, *can*, *could*, *would / do you mind if* … ?

Asking for permission			Responding
most formal ↕ least formal	**Would you mind if**	I used your phone?	No, not at all. / No, go ahead. Sorry, but …
	Do you mind if		
	May/Could **Can**	I use your phone?	Certainly. / Of course. Sure, no problem. / OK. Sorry, but …

- Use *May I, Could I,* or *Can I* to ask permission to do something.
- To ask for permission formally, use …
  - *Do you mind if* I + verb. →present
  - *Would you mind if* I + the past tense of the verb.

Note: To agree to a *Would / Do you mind if* … request, you answer with *No.* (= No, I don't mind.)

Lesson B   **Language Link:** Verb + gerund vs. verb + infinitive

I **need** to buy a new cell phone.	Certain verbs can be followed by an infinitive (*to* + verb).
I **avoid** talking on the phone when I'm driving.	Other verbs can be followed by a gerund (verb+ *-ing*).
I **like** to talk/talking on the phone.	Some verbs can be followed by an infinitive or a gerund. See p.112 for a list.

Unit 11   Technology Today

Lesson A   **Language Link:** *Used to*

Subject	*used to*	Verb		
I	**used to**	wear	glasses in high school, but I don't anymore.	*Used to* is a special past tense form. Use it to talk about things that were true or happened regularly in the past, but are not true or do not happen now.
	didn't use to		glasses, but I do now.	

Questions	Answers
Did you **use to** have long hair? **Did** they **use to** live in Tokyo?	Yes, I did. / No, I didn't. Yes, they did. / No, they didn't.

Lesson B Language Link: *As ... as*

Phone A costs $100. Phone B costs $100.
  Phone A costs **as** <u>much</u> **as** phone B.

Jon **isn't as** tall **as** his brother. (= His brother is taller.)

Russia **doesn't** have **as** many people **as** China. (=China has more people.)

My phone works as well as <u>your phone</u>.
  = My phone works as well as <u>yours</u>.

She studies as hard as <u>he studies</u>. (not common)
She studies as hard as <u>he does</u>. (common)
She studies as hard as <u>him</u>. (very informal)

You're as tall as <u>I am</u>.
You're as tall as <u>me</u>. (very informal)

Use *as* + adjective/adverb + *as* to show that two things are equal.

You can use *not as ... as* to show that things are not equal.

Sometimes after *as ... as*, you can end a sentence with a pronoun.

In spoken English, it's common not to repeat the verb after *as ... as*, but to say things as shown.

Unit 12 Let's Go Somewhere!

Lesson A **Language Link:** Modal verbs of necessity

	Present forms	**Past forms**
Affirmative	You **must** <u>show</u> your ID to get on the plane. I **have to** <u>buy</u> a backpack for my trip. We**'ve got to** <u>get</u> some cash.	I **had to** <u>wait</u> at the airport for an hour.
Negative	I **don't have to** <u>check</u> any luggage.	I **didn't have to** <u>wait</u> long.

- Use *must, have to,* and *have got to* + <u>the base form of a verb</u> to say that something is necessary.
- In spoken and written English, *have to* is used most commonly.
- *Must* is often used to talk about rules or laws. *Must* is stronger than *have (got) to*.
- Only *have to* can be used in the negative or to talk about things that were necessary in the past.

Lesson B **Language Link:** The present perfect for indefinite time

Present perfect	Simple past
I**'ve been** to Korea. He**'s taken** the driving test three times.	I <u>went</u> to Korea last year. He <u>took</u> the test in March, May, and July.

- Use the **present perfect** to talk about past actions when the time they happened is unknown or unimportant.
- When you mention a specific time (*last year, March*), use the <u>simple past</u>.

Questions	Answers	
Have you **(ever)** been to Brazil?	Yes, I have. No, I haven't. No, I've **never** been there.	*Ever* = at any time in the past up to now *Never* = at no time in the past
Have you packed **yet**?	Yes, I've **already** packed. (I'm done). Yes, I've packed **already**. No, I haven't packed **yet**.	Use *yet* or *already* to talk about whether an action has been completed. Use *yet* in questions and negative statements. Use *already* in affirmative statements.

Answers to page 70, Vocabulary, Activity A

1. becoming an adult **2.** wild **3.** a gift **4.** man's, him **5.** team **6.** before

Answers to page 113, Communication, Activity A

1. b **2.** a **3.** c **4.** b